Critical *i*nventions

General Editor: John Schad
Lancaster University

"a creative intellectual enterprise as rare as it is necessary in an academy which is now over-institutionalised and deadened by bureaucracy."
Jonathan Dollimore

John Schad is Professor of Modern Literature at the University of Lancaster. He is the author of *The Reader in the Dickensian Mirrors* and *Victorians in Theory*, the editor of *Dickens Refigured*, Thomas Hardy's *A Laodicean*, and *Writing the Bodies of Christ*; and co-editor of *life.after.theory*. His *Queer Fish: Christian Unreason from Darwin to Derrida* was published by Sussex Academic in 2004.

A depiction of confusion is not the same as a confused depiction.

Walter Benjamin, 'Central Park'

THE HABITS OF
DISTRACTION

MICHAEL WOOD

sussex
ACADEMIC
PRESS
Brighton • Chicago • Toronto

2 4 6 8 10 9 7 5 3 1

First published 2018 in Great Britain by
SUSSEX ACADEMIC PRESS
PO Box 139
Eastbourne BN24 9BP

Distributed in the United States of America by
SUSSEX ACADEMIC PRESS
Independent Publishers Group
814 N. Franklin Street, Chicago, IL 60610

British Library Cataloguing in Publication Data
A CIP catalogue record for this book is available from the British Library.

Library of Congress Cataloging-in-Publication Data
Names: Wood, Michael, 1936– author.
Title: The habits of distraction / Michael Wood.
Description: Brighton, [England]: Portland, Oregon : Sussex Academic Press, 2018. | Series: Critical inventions | Includes bibliographical references and index.
Identifiers: LCCN 2018005816| ISBN 9781845192495 (hbk : alk. paper) | ISBN 9781845192501 (pbk : alk. paper)
Subjects: LCSH: Benjamin, Walter, 1892–1940—Criticism and interpretation. | Barthes, Roland—Criticism and interpretation. | Distraction (Philosophy) Motion pictures—Philosophy. | Arts—Philosophy. | Interpretation—Philosophy.
Classification: LCC PT2603.E455 Z964 2018 | DDC 801/.95—dc23
LC record available at https://lccn.loc.gov/2018005816

Typeset and designed by Sussex Academic Press, Brighton & Eastbourne

Contents

Series Editor's Preface

As Michael Wood observes, for Walter Benjamin, 'even the distracted person can form habits'. Distraction has its habits, if you will. It is less mercurial than I think. More predictable than I think. More mappable. It may even be possible to write a book about distraction. This book for instance. A book in which, in short, distraction is shown to be itself a habit.

But is it, you ask, a good habit? Difficult to say. It may, it seems, be bad for you, very bad. Indeed, you may even die of it. Like the critic Roland Barthes. As Wood reminds us, Barthes once stepped off a sidewalk in Paris only to be hit by a laundry van. 'To be distracted from life,' remarks Wood, 'means to lose it.'

So, no, it perhaps may not be said that the habit of distraction is good for you. What, though, *can* be said is that Wood is good at the habit of distraction. Indeed, it is a habit he here turns into an art. But then, he has long been drawn to what he calls 'scenes of distraction,' artful scenes, such as jazz clubs and cinemas – and, yes, books, even (or perhaps especially) when they are being examined slowly, patiently, carefully. Literary criticism, we call it. As Wood here not only tells but shows, books most certainly can and should distract the literary critic. We critics may yet choose to become lost within our books. We may yet allow ourselves to go astray and to be thereby, as he says, citing another, 'at home in the world's scatter.'

And this is particularly so, it seems, if, like Wood, we dare to read closely – very closely. This, he shows, means, paradoxically, to *concentrate* on what distracts us, to fuss excessively over all the stray, marginal and unimportant details that really should not command our attention, and that we should ignore, banish from our thoughts, not be tempted by. But there is herein a risk, he warns. Such a concentrated-ly distracted form of close reading may in the end, if there is an end, 'an end to distraction,' as Wood says (hoping there is not), mean that we 'get too close.'

Too close to what?

Too close to stories. To be distracted, shows Wood, is to tell stories; we may return from distraction with *tales* not analysis

Too close to freedom. To be distracted, shows Wood, may entail freedom of a kind and an extent that we do not want.

Too close to defeat. To be distracted, shows Wood, may mean an end to the 'glory of our success,' the glory of our success as serious, admired, and tenured scholarly readers.

Too close to others. 'When we consider the habits a distracted person may form,' says Wood, 'we have to think of habits we may share with others.' We may, to our alarm, find ourselves, he says, among what Claudius in *Hamlet* calls 'the distracted multitude.' Close-up and impersonal, as it were. 'At the end of distraction,' says Wood, 'lies . . . sheer, new immediacy.' In short, he foresees a world, or scene without mediation – without, in particular, the mediation of conventional criticism, a mediation that keeps at a safe distance the worldly scatter of not only books but people, other people, all the other people, even those people who have nothing to do with universities. Allowing ourselves as critics to be distracted may, then, mean that we are, in the end, drawn out of the academy. Drawn out of its gilded cage. But then, as Wood says, 'cages are not everything.' Read on.

JOHN SCHAD, Series Editor
Lancaster, January 2018

The Critical Inventions Series

Do I dare / Disturb the universe?
(T. S. Eliot, 'The Love Song of J. Alfred Prufrock', 1917)

In 1961 C. S. Lewis published *An Experiment in Criticism*; over forty years later, at the beginning of a new century, there is pressing need for a renewed sense of experiment, or invention in criticism. The energies unleashed by the theoretical movements of the 1970s and 1980s have been largely exhausted – many now say we are experiencing life after theory; some, indeed, say we are experiencing life after criticism. Criticism, we might say, is in crisis. But that is where it should be; the word 'criticism' comes, as we know, from the word 'crisis'.

Talk of crisis does not, though, fit easily within the well-managed contemporary academy; with its confident talk of 'scholarly excellence', there is a presumption that we all know, and are agreed upon, what scholarship and criticism is. However, to echo Paul de Man, 'we don't even know what reading is'; and what is, potentially, exciting about our present crisis is that now we really know that we don't know what reading is. It is, then, in a spirit of learned ignorance that we propose 'critical inventions', a series which will feature books that, in one way or another, push the generic conventions of literary criticism to breaking point. In so doing the very figure of the critic will shift and change. We shall, no doubt, glimpse something of what Oscar Wilde famously called 'the critic as artist', or what Terry Eagleton called 'the critic as clown'; we may even glimpse still more unfamiliar figures – the critic as, for example, autobiographer, novelist, mourner, poet, parodist, detective, dreamer, diarist, flaneûr, surrealist, priest, montagist, gambler, traveller, beggar, anarchist . . . or even amateur. In short, this series seeks the truly critical critic – or, to be paradoxical, the critic as critic; the critic who is a critic of criticism as conventionally understood, or misunderstood. He or she is the critic who will dare to disturb the universe, or at least the university – in particular, the institutionalisation of criticism that is professional, university English.

Establishment English is, though, a strange institution that is capable of disestablishing itself, if only because it houses the still stranger institution of literature – which, as Jacques Derrida once wrote, 'in principle allows us to say everything/ anything [tout dire]'. We, therefore, do not or cannot yet know of what criticism may yet be capable – capable of being, capable of doing. 'Critical inventions' will be a series that seeks to find out.

Read the text right and emancipate the world.
(Robert Browning, 'Bishop Bloughram's Apology', 1855)

JOHN SCHAD, Series Editor

PART ONE

Out of Theory

They stared, and were distracted; no man's life
Was to be trusted with them.

William Shakespeare, *Macbeth*

ONE

The Distraction Set

I

'Where was I? Oh yes, I was writing a book about distraction,
and then . . .

Let me tell you about a dream I had not long after I started work on
the project. I was walking in the grounds of the Institute for
Advanced Study at Princeton with Walter Benjamin. He had been
dead for more than sixty years by this time, but the dream didn't
mind and I was delighted. He was very amiable, talked as if we were
old friends but also seemed rather . . . distracted. No, of course he
wasn't distracted, he was thinking of something else, more interesting
than the conversation. But then he *was* distracted – at least from our
conversation. This is where things get a little complicated. Are we
distracted if we are concentrating on the wrong thing? And who says
it's wrong?

As the dream continued, or became a new dream with the same cast,
it seemed to involve a funeral in Princeton, an informal gathering of
the dead person's friends, and a trip to Connecticut. The purpose of
the trip was not at all clear to me, but I have no doubt that my unconscious had its sources, and it occurs to me now that the words
'connect' and 'collect' may have been hanging around in the shadow-
lands of the dream – they would have been antidotes to the idea of
distraction.

Obviously the dream borrowed the notion from Benjamin himself and
got him to act it out. His friendliness was mere projection on my part.
I could lay no claim to sustained or intimate knowledge of his work,
but I had lived with fragments of it for a long time, and he was always
there when I needed him. A real friend in this sense, as the dream knew.

Benjamin doesn't have a theory of distraction, although he did leave a
fragment called just that. What he has is his essay 'The work of art in
the age of its technological reproducibility', and above all, within that

piece, a luminous, mysterious sequence of three paragraphs, the last of which contains the three remarks that form the basis of this book. I can't make them into a single coherent proposition, but I can try to follow out some of their implications and see where they lead. There is a 'life after theory', as John Schad says,[1] but many of its more interesting reaches may still represent stages on the way to what a theory might be.

The remarks are as follows. 'Even the distracted person can form habits'. A more idiomatic translation might be 'The distracted person can get used to things too'. Then, italicized by Benjamin himself: *'Reception in distraction – the sort of reception which is increasingly noticeable in all areas of art and is a symptom of profound changes in apperception – finds in film its true training ground'*. And finally, 'the audience [in the cinema] is an examiner, but a distracted one' [I 167/SW4, 268–269]. My plan is to ask what it means to form habits in the midst of distraction; to wonder how reception in distraction works both in the cinema and in other places; and to examine, insofar as it is possible, the examiner's distraction.

Another scene, not a dream this time. I was giving a talk in London. The date was 1998 and the topic was Hollywood cinema. The occasion was a seminar sponsored jointly by the *London Review of Books* and the *New Left Review*, two impeccably undistracted journals. The event was designed as something of a set-up. I would talk as an enthusiastic fan, and the distinguished audience would point out my lowbrow, untheorized errors. I thought this would be fun, but nothing of the kind happened. The members of the audience loved the movies as much as I did, and we all basked in our enjoyment. There was a difference, though, and this is where the thought of Benjamin came in. The audience believed great Hollywood movies were not actually Hollywood movies, they were critical or ironic versions of the form, that was how they rose above it, turned it into art. I certainly thought that some Hollywood movies were better than others (and some were and are terrible) but I thought the greatest were perfect examples of the form not deviations from it. We could say the friendly members of the audience were critics while I was a consumer, which was what the set-up was supposed to show after all. I found I wanted to say they were examiners who knew how to concentrate. I was, in Benjamin's terms, an examiner, but a distracted one. I had formed different habits and spent more time, perhaps, in distraction's training ground.

A particular instance of discussion was Clint Eastwood's western *The Outlaw Josey Wales*, a masterpiece by any standards. We all agreed there was plenty of irony and wit in the film, and that some of its best laconic lines ('Dyin' ain't much of a livin', boy') work as examples of the genre's intimate complication, where a virtually silent hero (in this film Eastwood mainly says 'I reckon so' and 'I reckon not') always has a few lines that make him sound like Lucretius or La Rochefoucauld. But I think that distraction teaches us – distraction from the particular case, and from a single, superior sense of irony – that genre of any kind often mirrors or contradicts itself. It just doesn't always do it so well.

One more leap in time, and then I'll stop miming distraction and settle down to talk about the textual Walter Benjamin, and not a phantom or a memory. Soon after Marlon James received the 2015 Man Booker Prize for his novel *A Brief History of Seven Killings*, I had a chance to put to him the question I had been wanting to ask ever since I read the book. Why did he have his Jamaican gangster call himself Josey Wales? James is a very literary writer who acknowledges Marguerite Duras in his afterword, and I suppose I expected some sort of cineastic equivalent in reply. He said when the street kids in Jamaica want to act tough they don't think of gangsters, real or imaginary, they think of westerns, and especially of Clint Eastwood westerns, and one stance or gesture in particular: the walk towards the enemy with hands poised over two guns still in their holsters. Not Josey Wales in particular then, and the name is not exactly an allusion. It is a glance at a pose, and one with an intriguing history: born in American westerns, but reborn into its most memorable form in the imagination of Sergio Leone and the figure of Eastwood the actor in Italian movies. This is the sort of co-production that makes the idea of intertextuality look impoverished, and that perhaps only a distracted mind could begin to map.

II

Let's start by looking more closely at Benjamin's argument. He pursues the term 'distraction' (*Zerstreuung*) partly in response to some remarks by the novelist Georges Duhamel, who had included an onslaught on the cinema in his witty and gloomy book on America, *Scènes de la vie future* (1930). Duhamel had said (in Benjamin's translation) that a film does not require any kind of concentration [*Konzentration*] or any capacity for thought [*Denkvermögen*] – Duhamel's own terms were *effort* and *suite dans les idées*. The first step Benjamin takes is to remind us of Duhamel's social prejudice. The masses seek entertainment and not art. Art requires concentration (effort, logic), and the masses aren't up to it. But this is just an 'ancient lament' and 'a commonplace', Benjamin says, implying that Duhamel dislikes the cinema because he dislikes the masses. We (assuming we are not members of the masses ourselves) don't have to enjoy everything the masses enjoy – even Benjamin is prepared to speak of the 'disreputable form' of some popular entertainment – but we do have to see that the world is changing, and that quantity doesn't necessarily ruin quality. It can become quality. 'The greatly increased mass of participants has produced a different kind of participation'. Indeed, Benjamin's claim throughout the whole essay is that art itself will change because of the newly developing modes of reception. Or has already changed. Even while carefully hanging on to many of the louche connotations of distraction Benjamin suggests it involves a genuine capacity for alternative attention. The concentrated connoisseur is 'absorbed by' the artwork, while 'the distracted masses absorb the work of art into themselves' [I 166/SW4, 267–268].

'The sort of distraction that is provided by art', Benjamin says, 'represents a covert measure of the extent to which it has become possible to perform new tasks of apperception' [I 167/SW4, 268]. We see that Benjamin is now talking about 'art' without qualification, not about entertainment; and what Zohn and Jephcott translate as 'true training ground' is more literally, and perhaps more interestingly, an actual or authentic instrument of practice, an *eigentliches Übungsinstrument*.

Duhamel, Benjamin says, 'detests the cinema and knows nothing of its significance, though he does know something about its structure' [I 164/SW4, 267]. Adducing another witness whose work hovers behind Benjamin's essay, we might suggest – we might imagine that Benjamin is quietly suggesting – that Siegfried Kracauer has understood something of the significance of distraction but nothing about its structure. This would be a little harsh, and would miss some of the irony and speculation in Kracauer's thought, but it might not be entirely wrong. What's interesting about Kracauer's essay on 'The Cult of Distraction' (1926) is his claim that distraction could meet a need other than the one it is supposed to meet. The new film palaces – these aren't movie-houses, Kracauer says, it would be disrespectful to call them that, movie-houses belong to the past and the suburbs – are in themselves, and offer as their wares, a sort of Wagnerian show for the

20th century: a *Gesamtkunstwerk der Effekte*. 'Distraction arrives in them at its own culture'.[2] We may note that Kracauer is not saying, as many have thought he was, that distraction *is* culture these days.

There are masses in the provinces, Kracauer says, but the tension of the working masses is stronger and more perceptible in Berlin than elsewhere. This is why people say Berliners seek distraction, or long for it, they are *zerstreuungssüchtig*. These people are right in what they see, wrong to make a reproach out of their observation: 'the reproach belongs to the petty bourgeoisie'. The members of the large bourgeoisie meanwhile, Kracauer suggests in a slightly later (1928) essay, get something quite different from the cinema: not distraction but delusion, a picture of themselves and their dreams. 'They have a reason not to know how they look in reality, and if they describe something as untrue, it is all the truer'. This is a tricky thought, but it becomes clearer through Kracauer's wonderful example: 'It may not easily happen in reality that a scullery maid marries a Rolls Royce owner; but it is not the dream of the Rolls Royce owner that scullery maids dream of rising to his social height?'[3]

What happens with the masses at the cinema is different, though. In this case the public *meets itself* at the movies, and the act of being distracted – distraction meets distraction, so to speak – has, Kracauer suggests, 'a *moral* meaning'. But then the movies and the moviehouses miss this meaning because they treat distraction as an end in itself, and finally are no different from the plays and theatres of old. Distraction, Kracauer says, is 'meaningful only as . . . an image of the uncontrolled disorder of our world', and we need forms of distraction that will aim radically at revealing rather than concealing what is broken or decaying in our social arrangements.[4] This is the task, the vocation of the spectacular movie palaces, the *Lichtspieltheater*, with which the essay began.

But can this happen? And would it still be distraction if it did? If Benjamin may be continuing a conversation with Kracauer on this subject, T. W. Adorno, a little later, is certainly taking up a conversation with Benjamin. He writes to him in March 1936 saying all kinds of complimentary things about the most recent draft of the 'Work of Art' essay. Adorno, perhaps surprisingly, likes the idea of using popular art to attack middlebrow art, but he thinks Schoenberg is as far from cultural respectability as anything the movies can provide. 'There is no one who will agree with you more than I when you defend *Kitsch* cinema against the quality film; but *l'art pour l'art* needs just as much defending'. However, he is not at all convinced by Benjamin's theory of distraction, because 'in a communist society, work will be organized in such a way that human beings will no longer be so exhausted or so stupefied as to be in need of distraction'.[5] This is a political version of Pascal's view of our spiritual plight: 'If our condition were truly happy we should not need to divert ourselves from thinking about it'.[6] As it is, for Adorno, even the masses are 'full of the worst bourgeois sadism' when they go to the cinema, and their laughter 'is anything but salutary and revolutionary'.[7] The masses are about as far as they could be from, in Benjamin's language, performing 'new tasks of apperception'.

Adorno and Duhamel, albeit from very different political places, refuse to see any sort of redemption in distraction. By way of filling out the cultural context, we might recall some of I. A. Richards' remarks in *The Principles of Literary Criticism* (1924):

> bad literature, bad art, the cinema, etc., are an influence of the first importance in fixing immature and actually inapplicable attitudes to most things . . .

> No one can intensely and wholeheartedly enjoy and enter into experiences whose fabric is as crude as that of the average super-film without a disorganization which has its effects in everyday life.[8]

This was in many ways the standard position of the time, the stock response to the idea of other people's stock responses – although the casual run of words 'bad literature, bad art, the cinema' is quite grand in its way.

Kracauer sees a possibility of redemption in distraction, but doesn't have much confidence in its becoming a reality. And his use of the word 'cult' in his title, although mainly mocking and picturesque, a sort of joke connecting cult and culture, points in exactly the opposite direction to that of Benjamin's work. The attraction of technical reproducibility for Benjamin is that it destroys the cult value of art, the sacred status of the unique art object. Photography and film, he wants to argue, make all the old hieratic and hierarchical assumptions about art unavailable or irrelevant. He was wrong about this, for historical reasons that belong to another discussion, but right to see the chance of such a change, as Kracauer saw the chance of entertainment's doing more than entertain.

But unlike Kracauer, Benjamin doesn't think distraction needs redeeming, he thinks it's as redeemed as it's going to be, and he inverts almost every element of the standard critique. Diversion, pastime, spectacle, distraction, immature attitudes, disorganization – these are all prejudicial misnamings of a new mode of reception, or at least a mode that is only now (in the 1930s) allowing itself to be understood rather than dismissed. It is one of the ways, for example, in which key figures of Benjamin's personal mythology – the flâneur, the gambler and the collector – can both find themselves and lose themselves. As Howard Eiland suggests in a fine phrase, 'All three are at home . . . in the world's scatter'.[9]

III

Benjamin's disagreement with Duhamel and Adorno is not an empirical one. He does not have a tested sociological basis for his argument about reception in distraction, he is describing a possibility where they are busy closing potential doors. His argument doesn't require less submissive or dull-witted audiences than their clichés project, only the chance that movie-goers see things that movie-despisers don't see.

And although Benjamin insists on the opposition between distraction and concentration, this is a temporary, functional distinction that needs dismantling almost as soon as it is in place. There is, in these beginnings of a theory, no distraction in any final, analytic sense, only a series of moods and responses that do not match traditional ideas of concentration. This is partly an effect of cinema itself, and one aspect of Benjamin's sense of distraction follows directly from Duhamel's notion that the cinema doesn't allow an audience any time to think, even supposing these sorry people had any thinking capacity to start with. Punning on the word *Leinwand*, meaning both canvas and screen, Benjamin says those who look at paintings can yield to a 'train of associations', while the audience in the cinema can't do this. No sooner have they seen the film image 'than it has already changed'. 'It cannot be fixed on' [I 164/SW4, 267]. Miriam Hansen suggests Benjamin is thinking of 'a type of cinema experience still patterned on the variety format',[10] where short films were interspersed with other entertainments, and she is surely right. But then we could think of an agility of mind in the audience, rather than a dull submission to time.

The historical reminder is important in another respect too. As Jonathan Crary says, 'If distraction emerges as a problem in the late 19th century, it is inseparable from the parallel construction of the observer in various domains'. Benjamin's opposition conceals a long collaboration: 'modern distraction can only be understood through its reciprocal relation to the rise of attentive norms and practices'.[11]

Further, as I have already hinted, it is important to hold on to, as well as complicate, the negative associations of distraction. They are part of the alternative mode of attention, in the way that the word 'obtuse', used in a similar fashion by Roland Barthes, is more helpful to us if we remember its stubborn, unseeing implications than if we forget or correct them.

Distraction, for Benjamin and in this book, names a cluster of behaviours and responses that play out in different lexical arrangements in different languages, but still can be seen as the same cluster. The most important issue here is perhaps the difference between the concept of *distraction*, which has similar meanings in English and all Romance languages – they include the notion of a withdrawal of attention, a redirecting of attention to something other than the indicated object, and in older uses, the idea of madness – and the concept Benjamin uses, *Zerstreuung*. It literally means scattering, and its opposite, translated into English as concentration, is *Sammlung,* gathering. A person who is concentrating is *gesammelt*, collected, as in the phrase *gesammelte Werke*, collected works. 'If you were looking for a dizzying joke on this topic you might turn to the subtitle of Hans Magnus Enzensberger's book *Mittelmaß und Wahn (Mediocrity and Illusion)*. 'Collected Diversions' is an elegant rendering of 'Gesammelte Zerstreuungen', but doesn't quite do the absurdist trick. We can see why a publisher wouldn't like 'Concentrated Distractions', and 'Gathered Scatterings' is surely worse. But the joke may help us to see how the swirl of meanings functions.

The adjective (also a past tense of the verb *zerstreuen)* is *zerstreut*, and that is what Benjamin's examiner is. It is because of the implication of scattering, I think, that Harry Zohn translated the word as 'absent-minded'. The most significant difference between *distraction* and

Zerstreuung perhaps is that a person who is *zerstreut* is not necessarily concentrating on anything, while a person who is distracted is often, however vaguely, attending to something else. The *Oxford English Dictionary* lists a remarkable meaning for the English word 'distractor', with a first noted use in 1951: 'Any of the incorrect options in a multiple-choice question, esp. one which is beguilingly plausible.'

In the face of such attentive cunning, we might think *Zerstreuung* was some kind of cousin of intellectual openness, a way of listening to half-heard voices, even a form of negative capability. This would be going too far, and we need to remember that one of the chief meanings of the German word, if we are not engaged with its most literal originary sense, is entertainment. Benjamin uses it to translate what Duhamel calls a *passe-temps*, a pastime, having previously, out of mischief or an indifference to fine points that aren't really fine, translated 'divertisse-ment' as 'pastime', *Zeitvertrieb.* And before Benjamin begins his discussion of Duhamel's claims, we also meet, only to lose it again almost immediately, the word *Ablenkung,* a more literal relative of the Latinate distraction, since it means 'leading away', offered here as the opposite of *Versenkung,* 'immersion' [I 164/SW4, 267]. This is the concept that Kafka evokes when he makes his eerie assertion: 'evil is that which distracts', *böse ist das, was ablenkt.* The aphorism perhaps needs to be taken together with the one that follows it in the notebook: 'Evil knows about good, but good knows nothing about evil'.[12]

Your head is probably spinning – I know mine is – at the thought of all these words that are so close to each other and so far away: distrac-tion, scattering, diversion, absence of mind, dissemination, pastime, entertainment, and a different sort of distraction. Perhaps the best way to steady ourselves is to spin a little more and come to rest.

The hunter Gracchus, in Kafka's story of that name, has died in an acci-dental fall. He boarded his ship of death, and set sail for the land where all is quietness, and the dead stay dead. But his ship lost its way, he never arrived, and now must sail the world forever. In the story he shows up in the town of Riva, is carried ashore, and receives a visit from the mayor. The mayor, confronted with a talking corpse, quite reasonably asks our hero if he is dead. Gracchus says, 'Yes, as you see'. The mayor does want to clear things up, though, and says, 'But you are alive too'. 'To some extent,' Gracchus answers, 'to some extent I am alive' too.[13]

What happened to the ship? Well, Gracchus says, there was 'a wrong turn of the wheel perhaps, a moment's absence of mind on the part of the helmsman, the distraction of my lovely native country, I cannot tell what it was'.[14] The mayor wonders whether Gracchus is in any way to blame for his condition. He was a hunter, Gracchus says. He hunted, is there anything blameable in that? The mayor thinks not, but still wants to know who is responsible for Gracchus' plight. 'The boatman', Gracchus answers promptly, and then abandons the subject.

A casual error, a moment of inattention causes eternal travel and travail. Gracchus can't isolate the cause of his terrible fate because the cause is so small, so ordinary. It's hard to die and it's hard to live, it seems; but it's easy to slip between worlds. No one is to blame for what happens, perhaps not even the master of death's boat.

Malcolm Pasley's 'absence of mind' is *Unaufmerksamkeit*; his 'distraction' is *Ablenkung*. Other versions give us 'inattention' and 'detour'. 'As you see', we are back in the territory of the Benjamin paragraph, spinning in the circle of what we might call distraction and its friends. It is because meanings migrate among the set that our topic can't really be defined simply by the word distraction, or whatever clings to the word in a particular language. The topic has to be what distraction can be taken to mean, and also what in other languages perhaps isn't quite distraction but something just as interesting.

The most intelligent work I know on the 'problem of distraction' is the book of that title by Paul North, and it is intriguing therefore that North finds Benjamin's notion of reception in distraction 'odd and somewhat indigestible'. He says 'the structure of the phrase itself' has its interest, but 'its form poses an obstacle to understanding'. '"Reception in distraction" cannot easily be received; at best it is a paradox, at worst nonsense'. The idea is hard to receive because distraction, in 'the common understanding' of the term, is the opposite of attention and therefore of any sort of reception. North's own subject is 'a different distraction', which he also calls 'primal distraction', the opposite not of attention but of thought itself.[15] Well, not quite its opposite, rather its limit or unimaginable end or enemy, and North brilliantly pursues its career though Aristotle, the French 17th century, and the work of Kafka, Heidegger and Benjamin himself.

But I want to stay with the common understanding, which includes some quite uncommon implications, and needs to understand itself better. The difficulty with all our current talk about distraction, from road signs ('Distracted driving kills') to Barack Obama's concerns about our culture ('President is wary of distraction') is that we are far too convinced that we know what it is. Part of the purpose of this book is to undo this conviction, and replace it with a better sense of the range of possibilities.

We could start by saying, with Benjamin, that distraction is the opposite of concentration but not of attention. It may itself be a form of attention, either to a single alternative object or to a range of scattered objects. Crary's 'reciprocal relation' is a form of entanglement, and the word 'attention', in its old and new uses, is a real busybody. We seek attention, we attract it, we fix it, we grab it, we hold it. We have an attention-span. We have a deficit. We stand to attention. Germans in the movies are always saying *Achtung*. It often seems as if attention is mentioned only when there is too much or too little of it. Perhaps it is like sanity: we don't talk of it when the dose is right.

Daniel Kahneman reminds us of the implications of our idiom 'pay attention', as if attention were a debt or cost or currency. 'You dispose of a limited budget'.[16] Perhaps the audience in the cinema freely gives its attention to a film, rather than coughing up the full price a concentrated examiner might insist on. After all, it has already paid for admission. I want to suggest too that distraction, in special cases, may actually be a form of concentration after all, but let's leave that notion for a later page.

IV

Some seven years after the discussion in London where I thought of Benjamin's idea of distraction as the answer to a puzzle, the resolution of different ways of looking at a Hollywood movie, I found myself at Harvard giving a talk about 'noise'. James Joyce's *Finnegans Wake*, I argued, was full of the noise of meaning, and the ostensible task of critical interpretation was to reduce it, or to prove that some of the meanings were just noise. I thought the occasion might be ideal for exploring the boundaries of failure in these matters, and I realize now that the metaphor of noise is everywhere in my thinking about distraction. I didn't realize then, or at least not straight away, that Benjamin was waiting in the wings again.

One of the *Oxford English Dictionary*'s definitions of 'noise' is 'irrelevant or superfluous information or activity, esp. that which distracts from what is important'. Webster has 'irrelevant or meaningless data or output occurring along with desired information'. What is important? What is desired? The moment we turn to *Finnegans Wake* we know we are in trouble.

'Life is a wake', the text says, 'livit or krikit' [Wake 55]. The invitation, we assume, is to take it or leave it, or live or croak it, or live it or creak it. It's not always livid and it's not usually cricket. But it is a wake. You can't wake if you don't sleep; you can't have a wake if someone isn't dead; and you can't leave a wake if your ship isn't moving. You see how easily things can get out of hand even with a simple declarative sentence.

Here is a brief (and very funny passage) that focuses these questions wonderfully. A character called Shem is said as a little boy to have dictated to all his little brothers and sisters the first riddle of the universe, well more exactly to have 'dictited to of all his little brothron and sweestureens the first riddle of the universe'. Shem has a cockney accent but his brethren remain Irish enough, since they are broths of boys, and his sweet sisters provide the soup tureens with an echo of the colleen about them. Shem asks

> when is a man not a man?: telling them take their time, yungfries, and wait till the tide stops . . . One said when the heavens are quakers, a second said when Bohemeand lips, a third said when he, no, when hold hard a jiffy, when he is a gnawstick and determined to, the next one said when the angel of death kicks the bucket of life, still another said when the wine's at witsends, and still another when lovely woman stoops to conk him, one of the littlest said me, me, Sem, when pappa papared the harbour, one of the wittiest said, when he yeat ye abblokooken and he zmear hezelf zo zhooken, still one said when you are old I'm grey fall full wi sleep, and still another when wee deader walkner, and another when he is just only after being semisized, and another when yea, he hath no mananas, and one when dose pigs they begin now that they will flies up intil the looft. All were wrong, so Shem himself, the doctator, took the cake, the correct solution being –

all give it up? –; when he is a – yours till the rending of the rocks, – Sham. [Wake 170]

This is not a difficult passage, as passages in *Finnegans Wake* go, and we get a lot of the fun straight away: the allusion to Balfe's *Bohemian Girl*, the gnostic (or agnostic) as a person who gnaws a stick and gets tarred, the idiom about kicking the bucket, the line from Goldsmith (or if you prefer, from *The Waste Land*), a popular music hall song ('When father papered the parlour'), the lines from Yeats ('When you are old and grey and full of sleep'), the English title of an Ibsen play (*When We Dead Awaken*), the joke about circumcision, the song 'Yes we have no bananas', the idiom about pigs flying, and the mention of the shamrock. But what are we to do with this, and how much are we missing? As Joyce's narrator asks, 'where in the waste is the wisdom' [Wake 114]? What sort of act of reading is asked of us, even supposing we have each managed to become, in Joyce's terms, 'that ideal reader suffering from an ideal insomnia' [Wake 120]? Should we perhaps go back to sleep?

We may want to say that in this sample and in *Finnegans Wake* more generally, everything is noise or everything is signal, and the two claims will then ultimately cancel each other out. Waste is wisdom and vice versa. That wouldn't make the claims useless, they could serve as provisional or therapeutic moves. If everything is noise, then the noise becomes the signal and we have to start again. Or just quit. And if we say everything is signal we have the rather daunting task of converting every piece of static into intelligibility. We could, in other words, learn from these immodest claims the very modesty they lack.

In practice I think we are always making deals with noise in *Finnegans Wake*: ignoring some of it, converting some of it into meaning, worrying about the patches we can't ignore and can't understand, enjoying some of it as noise. We need to keep in mind all the interpretative work still to be done even when we've got the gags about 'semisized' and 'circumsized', 'mananas' and 'bananas' and so on, and collected the allusions to Balfe, Goldsmith, Yeats and Ibsen.

And if we look at the passage again, we see that the riddle Shem poses is a fraud, the answer an elementary tautology. That's what really takes the cake and why he takes the cake. The answer to the question 'When is a man not a man' is: 'when he is not a man, when he is a sham man'.

(This is my accidental pun, not Joyce's, but you will understand why I decided not to censor it. It certainly arrived as noise but is it noise now?). Shem is a sham, and his early history proves it. To be sure, this is his brother's hostile view and not to be taken on trust, but for the moment there is nothing to contradict it. And if the right answer to the riddle is a non-answer, then perhaps we should pay attention to the wrong answers and see what we can find among them. The children give thirteen responses. The first three seem to suggest that a man is not a man (not a human or a humanist, perhaps) when he is religious: a quaker, a Bohemian protestant or an agnostic (or gnostic). After that the answers get more random: when he's dead; when he's drunk; when he's smitten with a woman; when he's at war or at sea; when he overeats; when he's old; when he's a ghost; when he's circumcized; when his time is up; when pigs can fly.

I'm not sure there's much of a pattern here, but even if there was we would be unwise to invest in it, because we are already missing too much. My account is not just a paraphrase or a drastic simplification, it's a hopeless double translation: into English and into something resembling rational argument. The text certainly presents these possibilities to us. Think of all the unaltered words in the passage, and the appearance of a narrative and numerical logic: 'One said . . . , a second said . . . , a third said . . . , the next one said', and so on. But it presents all kinds of other possibilities too, and it doesn't adjudicate among them. What do we make of the suggestion of thunder in 'the heavens are quakers', the suggestion of romance in the lips of the Bohemian girl (the song begins 'When other lips')? Does the phrase 'when the wine's at witsends' really propose anything as straightforward as just being drunk? The lingering idiom is 'when the wine is in the wit is out', but we could be at our wits' end because of too much or too little wine, and we might have wine at the end of our wits the way we have thoughts on the tip of our tongue. I don't really know what the phrase about pappa and the harbour means, and suggested at sea or at war because I thought of invasions of Ireland and of harbours being peppered. The song that's being adapted is rather more relevant to the novel in general, since it's about fixing up a house and falling down and it ends in a pub, but I don't know how to turn it into an answer to the riddle. When is a man not a man? When he's papering the parlour doesn't seem to do it.

Similarly, I don't really know what to do with the wild juxtaposition of Yeats and Apfelkuchen, and the strange bit of Dutch ('zo zhooken'). Joyce doesn't write, as Yeats did, 'when you are old and grey', he writes 'when you are old I'm grey'. This is more companionable, but hardly an answer to a riddle. What does having no mananas have to do, apart from the rhyme, with having no bananas? And should we pronounce the absent tilde?

Of course *Finnegans Wake* is full of puns that are more than puns. Sometimes the transpositions are breathtakingly simple, like 'while the sin was shining' or 'the late cemented Mr T. M. Finnegan', or the person who says he is 'selfthought' [Wake 385, 221, 147]. 'He urned his dread' [Wake 24] is rather different, since it turns ordinary work into a scary labour of doom, a process of accumulating, even commemorating terror.

There is great pleasure in seeing how wonderfully these 'significant' jokes work, but I don't think they provide the model we need for our reading. Not if it's our only model. It's too neat and functional, too economical, and it can easily cross over into a form of puritanism – as if we didn't like jokes that didn't earn their keep, or even put in over-time. And as a model for reading *Finnegans Wake* it fails us too often, because it effectively refuses the noise. It converts what it can into signal, and has to let the rest go.

What are we to do with the continuous, diverting, unconverted noise? When I first asked this question I hadn't read Michael Warner's remarkable essay on 'uncritical reading', which he calls 'the uncon-scious of the profession' – of the profession of the literary academic, that is.[17] He includes distraction among the uncritical modes of reading (along with identification, self-forgetfulness, reverie, sentimentality, enthusiasm, literalism, aversion), and I see now that I was looking for an alternative to conscious, commenting reading, for an uncritical reading that had its own touch of criticism or at least intellectual curiosity in it.

The richness of the following little rhyme seems to me both unmistak-able and unmanageable. 'Rockaby, babel, flatten a wall' [Wake 279]. The 'sources' are clear enough: two nursery rhymes and a biblical tower. The cradle on the treetop, destined to fall when the bough breaks at the end of the rhyme; the inhabitants of the ancient city building a tower that will reach the sky and make them a name; Humpty Dumpty who sat on a wall, and promptly fell off. But what about the curious fusion of baby and babel? We know God flattened a wall at Babel, but what does it mean to rhyme 'flatten a' with 'sat on a'? And what do we get when we put together all these motifs and altitude and instances of falling together? Can we put them together? Should we? It was around here that I thought of Benjamin. He wandered into my mind as if he really was my friend in the much later dream. His theory of distraction, it seemed to me, might be a manageable theory of unmanageability.

TWO

Staying Too Long

I

I don't wish to argue that distraction is not sometimes dangerous, or deeply undesirable. Roland Barthes died of it, in two senses. He didn't pay attention to Paris traffic and he gave up paying attention to life.

In February 1980, he stepped off a sidewalk and was hit by a laundry van. The mishap led to his demise, although we also learned that it was 'not the immediate cause of death, but favoured the development of pulmonary complications',[18] that is, the recurrence of complications that had been pursuing Barthes for his whole adult life. One obvious thought, widely circulated, was that he died of grief for his mother's death, which had occurred two and a half years earlier, or at least that this grief encouraged him to collude with his own dying. I doubt whether the sequence was so simple and clear, but it is true, as Michel Foucault said at the time, that 'people do not realize how much effort is necessary to survive in a hospital'.[19] Also true more generally that under difficult conditions one can live only if one really wants to. To be distracted from life means to lose it.

When Kafka reminds us that evil is distraction, or when he tells us the story of Gracchus, he is shifting urgencies of this kind to the centre of ordinary life, to the question of just getting through the day. Most uses of the word distraction and its friends avoid these extremes, even though many of them are inclined to speak of danger. Persons in charge of motor vehicles, including laundry vans, will find emphatic warnings in their manuals of instruction. One such text I looked at recently lists smoking, paying attention to your pet, adjusting car controls, looking away from the road, and cellphone use as significant causes of accidents. It also mentions being 'generally distracted or lost in thought'. 'Detaching from reality', the note says, 'can prove useful when recharging creative energies or simply taking a respite from a hectic day. However, doing so while driving can be fatal.' The note says nothing about listening to music or audiobooks. And just to return for a moment to our lexical circus, it is worth noting that 'generally distracted' and 'lost in thought' are excellent translations of the broader, uninflected meaning of *zerstreut,* as distinct from the particular distraction of one thought by another.

There are many contexts of this kind, and competitive sports offer good instances for thinking about the matter. A tennis commentator at the US Open says 'Djokovic was distracted by that'. 'That' was what Djokovic saw as a faulty call by a line judge. He had allowed it to linger in his head when the totality of his attention was needed for the next point. The other commentator, John McEnroe, a man who knows quite a bit about distraction, says Djokovic 'has to get those thoughts out of his mind'.

This region of distraction theory is where all the sermons come in, and where distracted persons are usually the others, all those who are not as disciplined and focused as we are: 'the distracted multitude', as Claudius says in *Hamlet.* We may think of W. H. Auden's fierce injunction:

> For no free exercise of the human mind is possible until man has learned
> to exclude the irrelevant distraction of his immediate environment and
> concentrate on the problem he is attacking. . . [20]

I like the way the emphatic notion of an irrelevant distraction half-leaves the door open to relevant distractions. Not what Auden meant, I imagine, but a good instance of how hard it is to close doors completely, especially when your idea of concentration involves an attack.

'Reading', David Ulin writes, 'is an act of resistance in a landscape of distraction'. This is almost mantra of the world where literacy is felt to be under threat, and Ulin doesn't fail to mention the enemy: 'the problem of technology, the endless distractions of the Internet'. However, he does at least have the grace to see himself as a culprit or victim as well an accuser: 'This is the nature of my distraction: the world is always too close to hand'. Distraction is part of his own 'inability to hold at bay the insistence of the world'. And one of his formulations catches quite a few of the real complications of the question: 'it is not contemplation we desire but an odd sort of distraction, distraction masquerading as being in the know'.[21] We can use distraction to persuade ourselves that we are concentrating – an extremely refined manoeuvre. We are still distracted, of course, but who is to say this?

The anxiety about distraction and the devotion to it, divided among different sets of people or residing confusedly within a single mind, testify to all kinds of social and psychological conditions, but in the light of Benjamin's suggestion that the distracted person can form habits and serve as an examiner, they invite us to think about all those occasions when the avoidance of distraction is neither a matter of survival nor a moral imperative but an interpretative strategy. Can we choose to be distracted? Yes and no, and both answers will return repeatedly in this book.

A good general response to the invitation is to wonder what we might learn from an openness to distraction that we cannot learn from an earnest loyalty to our disciplines of attention. The stress would fall on the limitations of what is supposed to be good for us, and on the chances of thought and perception offered by playing truant, by metaphorically going to the movies when we should be somewhere else. A colleague of mine, Yanie Fecu, suggests for example that the use of computers in the classroom is not a distraction but an impediment to distraction, to all the doodling and daydreaming we might do if we were not concentrating on e-bay or our email. Both sets of activities are forms of distraction from the point of view of the unfortunate teacher, but the first bears a relation to speculative thinking, and the second does not.

This is where Benjamin's suggestion that 'reception in distraction . . . finds in film its true training ground' makes a helpful reappearance, and where an exploration of Roland Barthes' notion of the obtuse will tell us a lot about our habits, including ones that we don't know how to indulge. The distraction that can harm us is not different from the distraction that may reveal new modes of understanding. The difference is not in the phenomenon but in the occasion.

II

Distraction is not a key word in Barthes' vocabulary, a verbal fact that reminds us that we are talking about a multilingual cluster or set rather than a single concept. But he is certainly drawn to the set, and significantly amplifies its range. His 'best ideas' come to him, he says, when he is with a person he loves and is thinking about something else: 'this is . . . how I best invent what is necessary to my work'.[22] He believes we should be able to raise our heads frequently when reading, that is, take our eyes off the page. He is interested in what is dispersed, thrown down, decentered. He writes of diversions, displacements, of going astray. Discourse, he reminds us, etymologically means running here and there. One of his cherished metaphors is that of things being *à la dérive*, adrift, which we could also translate as unmoored, errant, rudderless, sliding. Indeed there is a moment in *The Pleasure of the Text* where he seems to be actively courting the term 'distraction' – and finally refusing it, perhaps, because one of the main meanings of the French word is 'amusement' or 'entertainment', and he is certainly talking about something less manufacturable than that. 'My pleasure', he says

> can very well take the form of a drift. *Drifting* occurs whenever *I do not respect the whole*, and whenever, by dint of seeming driven about by language's illusions, seductions, and intimidations like a cork on the waves, I remain motionless, pivoting on the intractable bliss that binds me to the text (to the world). Drifting occurs whenever social language, the sociolect, *fails me* (as we say: *my courage fails me*).[23]

Barthes offers a beautifully elaborate version of what a slip might be (but usually isn't): 'Let us imagine that the scientific study of slips one day discovers its own slip and that the slip is a new, unheard of form of consciousness'.[24]

Barthes often suggests that the enemy of thinking is . . . thought. Thought here would be organized rationality and would have a distinctly French tinge – or would be tinged by a distinctly French mythology. *Je pense, donc je suis* would not mean I exist because I have a consciousness but I exist because I form coherent thoughts, and 'donc' would be the rather bullying key word in the sentence as its equivalent would not seem to be in other languages. Barthes' resistance to meaning, his longing for 'a world that would be exempt from meaning (as one is from military service)'[25] is a late chapter in the story that also includes Proust's suspicion of intelligence and Bergson's celebration of intuition. As I shall suggest, this story, and others like it, is much broader than any story of distraction is likely to be but it does form the context in which distraction needs to be understood.

In Barthes' early work rationality has a specific content and the content forms the problem. His master is Bertolt Brecht, the great dismantler of naturalistic illusion, and not only in the theatre. Brecht, more than anyone else in the mid twentieth century, reminded us that many supposedly natural distributions – of wealth, talent, intelligence, for example – are the result of social arrangements, and more importantly, that we do nothing about them because we take them to be natural, or near-enough to natural. 'Who wants to prevent the fishes in the sea from getting wet?' Brecht memorably asked.[26] Barthes' book *Mythologies* is based on this argument. Myths of culture, nation and politics are to be exposed, resisted; later Barthes would say deconstructed. The enemy is the 'sickening' stereotype, the 'cultural proverb';[27] and what Barthes repeatedly called the doxa – the doctrine at the heart of secular orthodoxy. John Sturrock has a good phrase for this practice. Barthes, he says, helped us to understand that 'society is a spectacle', and he did this 'by revealing to us some of the mechanisms by which it obscures its artificiality'.[28]

But with the Paris events of 1968 and Barthes's discovery that he was not as close to in spirit to the rebelling students as he and others thought he might have been, the ground changed a little, and Barthes began to understand that myths can certainly be shown to be mythical but can be replaced only by other myths. Something similar happened to the elegant distinction between fiction and myth that structures Frank Kermode's remarkable book *The Sense of an Ending* (1967): a myth might be a fiction that is ignorant of its own fictionality, but knowledge of this condition doesn't help as much as it might seem to. If anti-semitism was a myth for a Hitler and a convenient fiction for Goebbels, it's not at all clear that we should prefer Goebbels' view. A similar belated understanding hovers over Benjamin's ambition, in his work of art essay, to provide a lexicon that will not be helpful to fascism. There are no safe lexicons, no scriptures the devil cannot turn to his purpose. Use is meaning and not the other way round: a lesson we could have learned from Wittgenstein and J. L. Austin, and have had to learn from history. This is not to say we cannot combat myths; only that we need to understand our armory better, and shall perhaps, as Luis Buñuel claimed he was doing in his lifelong filmic onslaughts on the bourgeoisie, have to fight poison with poison.

All of this is a little too militant and directed to engage in an intimate way with distraction, even if the problem often looks like an excessive reliance on, or an excessive innocence about concentration. But Barthes' suspicion of meaning – not of a meaning or set of meanings, but of meaning itself and its systematic oppressions – returns us directly to our subject. Almost too directly, given the subject.

Barthes dreams of a language that would make a rustling noise, a sort of steady murmur rather than an articulation of sense. He says *le sens poisse à l'homme*, the presence of meaning makes us sticky, as if we had jam or toffee on our hands, and for one of his 'exemptions' he imagines it would allow us to 'hear in the distance a meaning . . . liberated from all the aggressions of which the sign . . . is the Pandora's box' [OC III, 1025, 275]. In *Empire of Signs* especially, he abounds in metaphors of what might happen to the process of signification, or is already happening to the process for the westerner in Japan: the sign withdraws, meaning is shaken, suspended; suffers an 'effraction', a 'peremption'. Japan for Barthes is the perfect fantasy world for all those haunted by excesses of (good) sense – that feature that no one, according to Descartes, ever thought he or she had too much of. We can't expect meaning to go away, and we are too schooled by it to be attracted to the merely meaningless. What we (westerners) want, and what we can find in Japan is a realm of meaning, a whole empire, that we can both acknowledge and ignore. 'The dream', Barthes memorably says, 'is to know a foreign (strange) language and yet not understand it'.[29]

It's worth pausing over Barthes' phrase *la diffraction sutile du signifiant*, the subtle diffraction of the signifier.[30] Saussure's terminology – the concept of the sign made up of signifier and signified – was common currency among structuralists and their descendants and regarded by many others as merely an artful way of saying what we knew already. But to take on the terms too eagerly or decide to do without them is to miss at least two opportunities for interesting thought. First, the signified was not a name for what was meant, the object or emotion referred to. The signified was internal to the sign, the mental counterpart of the noise or mark constituting the signifier: the idea of the mountain or jealousy or whatever. When a sign is working comfortably, we scarcely need to distinguish the signified from the referent: the coffee we had in heads when we ordered it turns quickly enough into a drinkable reality. However, in mistaken identities, or lies, the signifier and the signified are in perfect harmony, while the sign connects to the wrong referent. I said elm and thought of an elm tree, to use Wittgenstein's example, but the tree I pointed to was an ash.
And second, the signifier can always slip away from its customary or

intended signified and seek other company. This is what happens every time we make a pun. But for Barthes the slippage is also a chance of freedom, part of a discreet if disorderly and often accidental resistance to the hegemony of the well-behaved sign. And for Jacques Lacan the slippage becomes something like the verbal machinery of the unconscious. 'A dream has the structure of a sentence', as he famously said,[31] but the structure allows for many variations, cheating grammar with mutations of meaning. We might think that dreams are the headquarters of such deviations. They distract us with sliding signifiers so that we can worry about their unthinkable signifieds without waking up.

I thought at one time that Barthes' chief contribution to a theory of distraction, as distinct from his recurrent, hauntingly evoked preoccupation with it, was to be found in *Camera Lucida*, and specifically in the distinction between *studium* and *punctum* in viewing photographs. We look at an image, and we see what is there, think about it in the way we expect to think. What we feel, Barthes says, 'derives from an average effect, almost from a certain training'. His word for 'this kind of human interest' is '*studium*, which doesn't mean, at least not immediately, "study", but application to a thing, taste for someone, a kind of general, enthusiastic commitment, of course, but without special acuity' [CC 48/CL 26].

'The *studium* is of the order of liking, not of loving', Barthes says [CC 50/CL 27]. And with photographs that we like but don't love, that is all there is. But then with photographs we do love, something breaks into the *studium,* or breaks out of the image and into the viewer's consciousness, 'shoots out of it like an arrow, and pierces me' [CC 49/CL 26]. Barthes calls this wounding element the *punctum:*

> the word suits me all the better in that it also refers to the notion of punctuation, and because the photographs I am speaking of are in effect punctuated, sometimes even speckled with these sensitive points; precisely, these marks, these wounds are so many points. [CC 49/CL 26–27]

Without the *studium* there could be no *punctum*. But without the *punctum* there is no love, no visual and emotional adventure. The *punctum* could be almost anything, or rather, almost anything could play its part. For Barthes it is often a detail, whose 'mere presence changes my reading' [CC 71/CL 42]. But the detail has to be found by the viewer, not planted by the photographer. If details don't 'prick' him, Barthes says, 'it is doubtless because the photographer put them there intentionally . . . the detail which interests me is not, or least is not strictly, intentional, and probably must not be so' [CC 79–80/ CL 47]. 'The *studium* is ultimately always coded, the *punctum* is not . . . What I can name cannot really prick me. The incapacity to name is a good symptom of disturbance' [CC 84/CL 51]. And finally, and perhaps most interestingly, 'the *punctum* . . . is an addition: it is what I add to the photograph and *what is nonetheless already there*' [CC 89/ CL 55, Barthes' italics].

There is much to think about here, because the claims are so suggestive, and because so many undeclared assumptions (we might say mythologies) are in play. The *studium* is obviously the habit of a straw self, the conventional other we all have within us. It does the sums and picks up the references, takes all our exams for us, but we have no wish to identify ourselves with its boring competence. But then the disturbance or the wound seems a bit too perfectly unprogrammed, as if defeating the system were more important than the occasion of escape. The role of the unintended here seems triply problematic: because we cannot be sure that the photographer did not intend the detail that pricks us, because in the instances Barthes cites the photographer almost certainly did intend the detail – the two nuns did not just wander into Wessing's picture of soldiers in Nicaragua – and because the event of the *punctum* happens in the viewer. Intention here plays the role of voluntary memory in Proust: it's not just that it doesn't capture the past, it can't. The doctrine allows us to feel free from intention when we are free only from an awareness of intention.

The same goes for the incapacity to name. It is a good symptom of disturbance, but Barthes has made it into a necessary condition of the *punctum*. Proust's mythology is behind this proposition too. 'What intelligence gives us back under the name of memory is not it' [CSB 211], he writes, and the proposition hovers, as do so many of Barthes' remarks, between shrewd perception and dogmatic aphorism. What intelligence frequently, perhaps always fails to do becomes what it cannot do by definition.

Still, the *studium* does, happily, break down, and concentration, in Benjamin's terms, is enhanced by distraction. It's just that, in my reading, Barthes' distraction is often a little too willed. The distracted examiner is more an examiner than he is distracted. The real interest of Barthes' distinction lies elsewhere, and although it speaks to distraction, it also shifts the ground.

Camera Lucida is a work of mourning as well as a book about photography. If certain photographs speak to us more than others, if certain details wound us, it is because, in photography as in no other medium, we can, as Barthes says, add to an image something the image already contains. We can add, the book suggests in its ongoing argument and its most poignant details, our own wonderment that what was once there, in the world – this person, this building – is still here, in this picture.

This formulation is the reverse of Barthes's famous paraphrase of what a photograph of a person says to us: 'that is dead and that is going to die'. 'In front of the photograph of my mother as a child, I tell myself: she is going to die' [CC 150/CL 96]. We import what was once a future into the past, and we lose our loved one again. Photographs are like the narrator's memory of his grandmother in Proust – Barthes himself makes this connection. An involuntary memory tricks the dead lady back into life, and only then does the narrator realize how dead she is. But the surprise of the photograph – Barthes finds in a single image and in no other 'the truth of the face I had loved' [CC 106/CL 67] – is real too, and we remember the marvelous memory that opens the book. Barthes sees a photograph of Napoleon's youngest brother, taken in 1852, and thinks 'I am looking at eyes that looked at the Emperor' [CC 13/CL 3].

At the heart of *Camera Lucida* both death and resurrection are superseded by the far more desperate need to believe – no, to possess a proof – that a now vanished person once existed. In this light a certain naïveté about photography ('Every photograph is a certificate of presence' [CC 135/CL 87) pales in significance compared to the portrait of an obsessed desolation, of a mind for which the time of a mother's 'unique being', is not only lost but threatened with cancelation. What Barthes needs to remain of his mother is not her identity – he can remember that – but her 'truth'. He knows *who* she was; needs the magic of photography to be sure *that* she was.

III

Barthes' opposition of the *punctum* to the *studium* is a development of a structure he elaborated in an essay called 'The Third Meaning', first published in the *Cahiers du cinéma* in 1970. The later work is a simplification as well as an intensification. Our viewing of a photograph we love, or even, perhaps, of any photograph that matters to us in a personal way, is the scene of a duel between what we know we ought to see (know how to see) and what we can't not see (and do not know how to manage). He can't show us the picture of his mother as a child, he says, because 'at most it would interest your *studium*: period, clothes, photogeny; but in it, for you, no wound' [CC 115/CL 73]. The wound is certainly a distraction from what Barthes calls the banality of the *studium,* but then becomes a grand new subject all of its own. It is a genuine distraction in one of the important senses of the English and French words, but it completely lacks *Zerstreuung*, any sort of feeling of scattering or diffusion.

It would be absurd to look to the *Cahiers* essay for the pathos and haunted passion of *Camera Lucida*, for an account of what Barthes calls the madness of photography, but if we seek an exploration of a mode of reading that includes the full range of what I have called the distraction set, 'The Third Meaning' is a textual treasure, as Barthes said of the Marx Brothers' *Night at the Opera*. He is almost certainly not thinking of Benjamin, but clearly amplifies and enriches Benjamin's suggestions – all the more clearly, as Barthes would no doubt say, because this was no part of his plan.

Barthes is looking at 'several Eisenstein stills' – the French word is *photogrammes*, like telegrams only written with light rather than from a distance [OCII, 867/RF 41]. His first example is the opening scene of *Ivan the Terrible*, and Barthes distinguishes three levels of meaning in the image. There is a level of communication, involving everything the image is trying to tell us about its setting, its story, its people. There is a level of signification, by which Barthes means the work of whatever conventional symbolism is present in a scene: gold, ornate clothing, elaborate ceremony as intimations of opulence, majesty, power, for example. And then there is a third meaning: 'I do not know what its signified is, at least I cannot give it a name, but I can clearly see the features – the signifying accidents of which this heretofore incomplete sign is composed'. As provocations of this meaning, Barthes names the courtiers' make-up, the 'stupid' nose of one, the fine eyelids and affected hairstyle of another [OCII, 868/RF 42–43]. Are his eyes wandering, or is he perceiving something that the first and second meanings cannot contain or cover? Barthes decides to call this level of interpretation 'signifying' [*signifiance*] – we might say meaning caught in the act rather than finally delivered [OCII, 868/RF43].

Barthes says he is not concerned with the first meaning (communication), only with the second and the third (signification and signifying). The second meaning is doubly determined, he says. 'It is intentional . . . and it is selected from a kind of general, common lexicon of symbols' [OCII, 868/RF43]. He calls the complete sign, the composite of the first two meanings, '*the obvious meaning*' [OCII, 868/RF44,] Barthes' italics]. *Obvie* is not the most familiar French word for 'obvious'. 'In theology', Barthes says, 'the obvious meaning (*le sens obvie*) is the one "which presents itself quite naturally to the mind"' [OCII, 868/RF44]. The third meaning, by contrast, is 'both stubborn and fugitive, apparent and evasive' [OCII, 868/RF44, translation slightly modified]. This is the second time he uses the word 'stubborn' (*têtu*) in this essay, a subtle effect since he is about to call the third meaning 'obtuse'. We find him resorting to this term in an interesting context late in his life:

> I love, not who he is but that he is. The language in which the amorous subject then protests [against all the nimble languages of the world] is an obtuse language: every judgment is suspended, the terror of meaning is abolished. [OCIII, 666]

But his use of the word in 'The Third Meaning' is the most elaborate and fully unfolded:

> This word readily comes to my mind, and miraculously, upon exploring its etymology, I find it already yields a theory of the supplementary meaning; obtusus means blunted, rounded . . . An obtuse angle is greater than a right angle . . . . the third meaning, too, seems to me greater than the pure perpendicular, the trenchant, legal upright of the narrative, it seems to me to open the field of meaning totally, that is infinitely. I even accept, for this obtuse meaning, the word's pejorative connotation: the obtuse meaning seems to extend beyond culture, knowledge, information. Analytically, there is something ridiculous about it; because it opens out onto the infinity of language, it can seem limited in the eyes of analytic reason. It belongs to the family of puns, jokes, useless exertions; indifferent to moral and aesthetic categories

(the trivial, the futile, the artificial, the parodic), it sides with the carnival aspect of things. [OCII, 868–869/RF 44]

This sounds like the manifesto of the really distracted examiner. There is also an impressive antecedent for this kind of thinking in Kierkegaard, cited by Marina van Zuylen.[32] The writer cannot concentrate on the boring conversation of a man he has to listen to: 'On every occasion, he was ready with a little philosophical lecture that was extremely boring'. However, the man did sweat a lot.

> This perspiration now absorbed my attention. I watched how the pearls of perspiration collected on his forehead, then united in a rivulet, slid down his nose, and ended in a quivering globule that remained suspended at the end of his nose. From that moment on, everything was changed; I could even have the delight of encouraging him to commence his philosophical instruction just in order to watch the perspiration on his brow and his nose.[33]

After a paragraph on the obvious meaning ('the obvious meaning is always, in Eisenstein, the Revolution' [OCII, 872/RF47]), showing that eloquent images of grief and anger may be powerful because 'Eisenstein's "art" is not polysemous' [OCII, 869/RF45], because nothing about them leaves their meaning in doubt, Barthes turns to his real subject. His starting point is a shot from *Battleship Potemkin* showing an old woman's face as she weeps. 'What is it', he asks, 'that raises the question of the signifier for me?' The 'full signification' ('closed eyelids, drawn mouth, fist over the breast') is part of 'the gestural repertoire of grief', moving as it is meant to be, but obvious. 'I felt', Barthes continues, 'that the penetrating feature – disturbing as a guest who persists in staying at a party without uttering a word, even when we have no need of him – must be located in the area of the forehead: the kerchief had something to do with it' [OCII, 872/RF47–48]. This hunch is confirmed by the next still. The same woman has her eyes and mouth open and the image, more insistent in its mood, leaves no room for indirection. The kerchief is there but takes up less space, because she has tilted her head backwards slightly; the forehead is no longer a focus. 'The obtuse meaning vanishes, there is no more than a message of grief' [OCII, 872/RF48]. It's worth pausing over the genuine obtuseness of this complaint: 'no more than', what does he want? We realize at once that more grief means more intended meaning, and therefore a limit on the viewer's freedom of interpretation. Barthes wouldn't want us to miss a certain irresponsibility in the idea of such freedom, just as Benjamin would not want us to think only of the virtues of distraction. What has happened between the two shots?

In the first there is a 'supplement or deviation imposed upon [a] classical representation of grief' [OCII, 872/RF48]. We don't have to see this supplement as Barthes does, or indeed see it at all, to understand what he means. If we don't see the supplement here, we shall see it elsewhere, and no doubt already have. Barthes finds that the closeness of the kerchief to the eyebrows, the angles of the woman's features ('the circumflex accent formed by the old, faded eyebrows, the excessive curve of the lowered eye-lids . . . and the bar of the half-open mouth') belong to the language not of grief but of 'a rather pathetic disguise' [OCII, 872/RF48]. 'The characteristic of this third meaning – at least in Eisenstein – actually blurs the limit separating expression from disguise' [OCII, 872/RF48].

Barthes goes on to discuss further instances of disguise in Eisenstein: a rather too prominent beard that 'calls attention to itself as false yet nonetheless refuses to abandon the "good faith" of its referent'; a 'hank of hair' in close-up that is 'ridiculous' as an expression of grief; a too large chignon that makes a woman look touching rather than militant [OCII, 873/RF49]. 'The obtuse meaning carries a certain emotion' – but not the obviously intended emotion.

> Such obtuseness transcends the anecdote, it becomes the blurring of meaning, its deflection . . . The obtuse meaning is not in the language system (even that of symbols). Remove it and communication and signification remain, circulate, pass . . . There are obtuse meanings not everywhere (the signifier is a rare thing, a future figure) but somewhere . . . [OCII, 873, 878/RF51, 54]

Barthes compares the 'aberration' of his own readings to the interest of 'the unfortunate Saussure' [OCII, 878/RF55] in anagrams no else saw or cared about, and as I am rereading his sentence I have a sudden flash of memory.

I am in a seminar room at Columbia in the 1970s, listening to a colleague, Sylvère Lotringer, talk about Saussure's work on anagrams. The assumption of most people in the room is that if this apparent craziness is Saussure's, it isn't craziness. Theory was a serious affair in those days, especially when we didn't understand it. The person sitting next to me is doodling on a piece of paper, which after a while he passes it to me. I can't remember the sentence written on it, but it was clearly an anagram of Sylvère Lotringer's name. I took this joke to represent skepticism – anagrams, unlike Barthes' obtuse meanings, are every-where – but didn't, until now, think of it as also the work of a distracted examiner.

Barthes goes on to say that 'the obtuse meaning is a signifier without signified; whence the difficulty of naming it'. It is 'outside (articulated) language, but still within interlocution' [OCII, 878/RF55]. But then he concentrates for a long paragraph on what the obtuse meaning acts against – 'the obtuse meaning is clearly the epitome of counter-narra-tive' [OCII, 880/RF57] – so that the orthodoxy of the world of replete signs becomes his real subject. 'What the obtuse meaning disturbs, sterilizes, is metalanguage (criticism)'. It is 'discontinuous, indifferent to the story and to the obvious meaning'. 'Ultimately the obtuse meaning can be seen as an *accent* . . . marking the heavy layer of infor-mation and signification' [OCII, 880/RF55–56]. It

> subverts not the content but the entire practice of meaning. A new –
> rare – practice affirmed against a majority practice (that of significa-
> tion), the obtuse meaning inevitably appears as a luxury, an expenditure
> without exchange; this luxury does not yet belong to today's politics,
> though it is already part of tomorrow's. [OCII, 880/RF56–57]

The rest of the essay argues that 'the third meaning structures the film differently [or structures film differently]', allows us to perceive the 'filmic', which 'begins only where language and articulated meta-language cease' [OCII, 881–882/RF58]; and that the still is the only place where we can see the version of itself that moving film hides. In *Camera Lucida* Barthes says 'I decided that I liked Photography in oppo-sition to the Cinema, from which I nonetheless failed to separate it' [CC 13/CL3]. But in 'The Third Meaning' he was already managing to separate cinema ('language, narrative, poetry') from film, which 'like the text, does not yet exist' [OCII, 882/RF59]. A still offers an announcement of this possible existence.

This is wonderful stuff and there is much to be said for thinking of the escaped signifier as the messenger of a new mode of meaning, but in their quarrels with official interpretations and mere 'cinema', the later parts of the essay lose some of the richer dimensions of the idea of the obtuse. To be discontinuous, indifferent, blurred, deflected, or a luxury, is precisely not to form a counter-narrative, or act coherently against a majority practice, and the essay's earlier claims are more varied and disorderly than its concluding combats.

What is important is that there is no analytic argument in the essay at all, only a series of metaphors, starting with geometry and ending with mental modes of resistance. To list for convenience only a few of the figures we have already seen, Barthes writes of angles, legality, stubbornness, ridicule, jokes, carnival, disguise, a guest at a party, forms of punctuation, a blur. When he says the obtuse is 'outside language', he doesn't mean we can't talk about it. He means we can only show it, as Wittgenstein said of what is mystical. There is nothing mystical about the obtuse, though. Our ability to see it, to experience our version of it, depends solely on the aptitude of our imagination, our willingness to make sense of these metaphors, or rather to take up the story they tell and do something with it. This is what Barthes means by his suggestion of a realm that is outside language but within interlocution, a place where names vanish but talk continues.

THREE

Something is Happening

I

Do we live in an age of distraction? The question perhaps is rather whether anyone has not lived in such an age – whether an age has ever existed that was not too distracted for some. 'Jeremiads against distraction', Miriam Hansen says, 'are as old as Pascal's rejoinder to Montaigne', of which we have already seen are a part.[34] Or even older. Bernard of Clairvaux, who lived between 1090 and 1153, disapproved of figures on church or chapel pillars because they might distract the monks – hence the plainness of Cistercian architecture. I thought there might even be Jeremiads against distraction in the *Book of Jeremiah*, but this turned out to be a limit case. The delinquents on that occasion were really concentrating on getting things wrong.

The complaints of Duhamel and Richards seem pretty old now. They were not groaning about the Internet or email or multitasking but about the movies, that now classic, even antique art form. However, there is a particular, modern history of the interest in distraction, and I want to trace some pieces of it before turning, in the second part of the book, to some practical experiments in the modes of interpretation I am trying to learn from Benjamin and Barthes. Much of the recent history of thought for both of these writers begins with Marcel Proust, and conveniently for us, Proust himself begins with Ruskin.

'The eye is continually influenced by what it cannot detect', Ruskin wrote in *The Stones of Venice*. 'Nay, it is not going too far to say, that it is most influenced by what it detects least'.[35] I don't think many people now will find this proposition surprising. We've had more than a century's worth of advertising to persuade us of the existence of hidden persuaders, and we've heard a lot about the unconscious. Still, the influence of the undetectable on the eye, as distinct from the mind or our behaviour is a fairly strange proposition. Ruskin is not thinking, as Poe's Arsène Dupin was, of peripheral vision or sidelong glances – a mode we could translate perhaps into lateral understanding. Nor is he making the distinction another famous detective was fond making of between seeing and observing. 'You have not observed,' Holmes says to Watson. 'And yet you have seen . . . I have both seen and observed'.[36] Ruskin is saying something altogether more mysterious . We don't see what we see. Or we see it but we don't detect it – precisely the opposite of Holmes, and still more the opposite of Watson, who on Ruskin's model isn't seeing anything.

Ruskin wasn't talking of hidden persuaders or the unconscious or a world of clues, he was talking about certain architectural details of St Mark's Cathedral in Venice. The portico offers, he says,

> an irrefragable proof of an intense perception of harmony in the relation of quantities . . . a perception which we have at present lost so utterly as hardly to be able even to conceive it. And let it not be said . . . that what is not to be demonstrated without laborious measurement, cannot have influence on the beauty of the design. The eye is continually influenced by what it cannot detect; nay, it is not going too far to say, that it is most influenced by what it detects least. Let the painter define, if he can, the variations of line on which depend the changes of expression in the human countenance. The greater he is, the more he will feel their subtlety, and the intense difficulty of perceiving all their relations, or answering for the consequences of a variation of a hair's breadth in a single curve. Indeed, there is nothing truly noble either in color or in form, but its power depends on circumstances infinitely too intricate to be explained, and almost too subtle to be traced.[37]

This is a very dense passage, driven by its analogies, and not strong on logic. The 'perception' seems at first to belong to the viewer then to the artist (builder, painter). We have utterly lost this perception, or perhaps we never had it, it was only an intuition of everything we were not going to be able to say we specifically saw. There is definitely a 'power' in such work, though, which touches us in spite of, or independently of, our inability to explain or trace or measure it.

In his remarkable book *Fateful Beauty* Douglas Mao quotes a piece of the Ruskin passage, and writes of 'the extraordinary depth of this period's interest in unregistered experience' – a very precise phrase. The period in question runs from the 1870s into the late 20th century, and the depth of this interest is indeed extraordinary. Mao discusses what he calls, in another fine phrase, Oscar Wilde's 'developed inattention to beauty'; and quotes Edith Wharton on 'unconscious cultivation', everything we learn without knowing we have learned it.[38] The interest is so deep that by the time we have moved from Ruskin to Proust only unregistered experience counts as real. And following Proust two of his best and most devoted readers, Walter Benjamin and Roland Barthes, find themselves developing, respectively, a defence of distraction and a notional 'third meaning', unavailable to any reputable mode of interpretation, however skillful or inventive.

For Proust, the very attempt to register experience kills it off, turns into it a hollow record, an inert catalogue of information. The shadow of Freud hovers here for all kinds of reasons, but he wasn't actually interested in unregistered experience. He was interested in experience that had a secret register, that hid itself away from our consciousness, and pounced on us in the form of symptoms. Still, the line between the absent register and the secret one will often seem a thin one. A more important line, perhaps, will be the one between the emphasis in Proust (and Barthes) on the negative power of conscious thought and the emphasis in Ruskin and (Benjamin) on the positive promise of the unintellectual examiner. Proust and Barthes, we might say, are seeking an escape from the dominion of training, from a culture of concentration; Ruskin and Benjamin are making the first moves towards a new education, a culture of distraction.

'Every day I attach less value to the intelligence', Proust's projected preface to *Contre Sainte-Beuve* begins [CSB 211]. By intelligence he means the whole range of intentional, functional thought, and the failure of this faculty is often a failure of seeing – a failure to detect what is seen, in Ruskin's terms. In one of the most spectacular, although rather neglected moments in *A la Recherche* a cluster of three trees appears during a drive the narrator takes with Mme de Villeparisis, a friend of his grandmother's, in the countryside around Balbec. The narrator wonders where he has seen the trees before. Not near Combray, he thinks; and not near the German spa he once visited with his grandmother. Perhaps in some place in his past of which no other trace remains. Perhaps in an old dream, or even a very recent one, 'a dream of only the night before, but already so faded that it seemed to derive from much longer ago'. Perhaps he has never seen them, perhaps their hidden meaning only feels like a memory. Perhaps it's just an effect of déjà vu.

I could not tell . . . I watched the trees as they disappeared, waving at me in despair and seeming to say, 'Whatever you fail to learn from us today you will never learn. If you let us fall by this wayside where we stood striving to reach you, a whole part of your self which we brought for you will return for ever to nothing'. And it is true that though the same mode of pleasure and disquiet which I had just experienced once more was to come back to me in later years, though I did attend to it at last one evening—too late, but for ever— I never did find out what it was these particular trees had attempted to convey to me, or where it was that I had once seen them. When the carriage went round a corner, I lost sight of them somewhere behind me; and when Mme de Villeparisis asked me why I looked so forlorn, I was as sad as though I had just lost a friend or felt something die in myself, as though I had broken a promise to a dead man or failed to recognize a god. [Recherche II, 78–79/Search II, 298–299]

What the missed message or memory stands for is the whole world of vivid sensation the intelligence cannot hold or store for us. It is the opposite of daily, practical life, it is lived life itself, what Proust's narrator calls 'our true life, our reality as we have experienced it' [Recherche IV, 474/Search VI, 189]. 'Experienced' means lived but forgotten; or rather, preserved in one form of memory because forgotten in the other. In the drastic fairy-tale that is *A la recherche du temps perdu* only chance, or distraction, can unlock this involuntary memory for us, which means we may never reach it, as Proust's narrator indeed will never know what the trees were trying to say to him. 'Too late but for ever' is his way of saying how much we miss even when time is regained; of reminding us that distraction cannot be counted on.

We do not perceive reality as we live it, Proust says in his early novel *Jean Santeuil*, we find it again as long as we do not look for it, 'in the sudden recall of a gust of wind, of a smell of fire, of a low, flat, sunny sky, close to rain, above the roofs'.[39] The intervention of chance, or the slackening of the concentrated will, is essential. This is where an alternative memory appears, and in *A la recherche du temps perdu* it delivers a series of redemptive experiences in which intelligence and intention supposedly had no part at all. One of them arises, conveniently for the theme of this book, when the narrator 'distractedly' – Scott Moncrieff renders renders *distraitement* as 'carelessly' while Ian Patterson has 'absent-mindedly' – opens a copy of a book that was important to him in his childhood [Recherche IV, 461/Search VI, 191].

The most famous of the experiences is the episode of the madeleine which appears near the beginning of *Du côté de chez Swann*, the most conclusive of them the set of instances that hurries into the pages of *Le Temps retrouvé*. The narrator's response in each case is the same: baffled, delighted immediate sensation, patient search for the elusive source, final finding of the connection. His solution to 'the riddle of happiness' the events offer is that the collision of times, the meeting of past and present in a sensation that belongs to both, reveal the continuing existence of an extra-temporal self, a creature who is fully alive both now and then. 'One minute freed from the order of time has recreated in us, in order to feel it, the man freed from the order of time' [Recherche IV, 451/Search VI, 181]. This is why he no longer feels 'mediocre, contingent, mortal' [Recherche I, 44/Search I, 47].

But a minute freed from time is itself still a minute, countable as time, and Proust doesn't fail to notice this. 'Fragments of existence' may escape temporality, but only temporarily: 'the contemplation of them, while a contemplation of eternity, was itself fugitive' [Recherche IV, 454/Search VI, 183]. And the narrator's long meditation on time and the self, and on the novel he is about to write, ends with a startling reappearance of the historical world in which no one is recognizable because everyone has aged so much. He calls this 'a dramatic turn of events . . . which seemed to raise the gravest of objections to my undertaking' [Recherche *IV*, 499/Search VI, 229].

Proust's critics, with a few distinguished exceptions, have until recently been so devoted to the happy end of the great novel that they have not wanted to think about these objections, or indeed about the many memory experiences in the text that point in quite different directions, but by the end of his essay on Proust Benjamin has developed his own very particular view of what involuntary memory means.

II

Benjamin reminds us that *A la recherche du temps perdu* is governed not by the author's experience but by the 'weaving of his remembering, the Penelope-work of memory'. He follows this analogy with two remarkable questions:

Or should one not rather speak of a Penelope-work of forgetting? Does not the involuntary memory, Proust's *mémoire involontaire*, stand much closer to forgetting than to what is usually called remembering? [I 335–336/SW2:1, 238]

Benjamin completes (and further complicates) his thought by an elaborate development of the figure of Penelope's tapestry. Remembering and forgetting are the warp and woof of the fabric of involuntary memory, but Penelope is a counterpart to Proust rather than a likeness, because Penelope undid at night the work she had completed during the day. With Proust the day itself undoes the work of the night, and in the morning we hold in our hands only 'a few fringes of the carpet of lived existence, as woven into us by forgetting' [I 336/SW2:1, 238].

Proust's eternity, Benjamin says, is limited time not boundless time – he doesn't even bother to exclude the possibility of the timeless. Life itself is an interplay of (voluntary) remembering and aging, and the miracles of involuntary memory, even as they literally rejuvenate us, make the world older. Benjamin quotes Baudelaire's 'Le Voyage' – 'Ah! que le monde est grand à la clarté des lampes!/Aux yeux du souvenir que le monde est petit!' – and comments:

Proust has brought off the monstrous feat of letting the whole world age a lifetime in an instant. But this very concentration, in which things that normally just fade and slumber are consumed in a flash, is called rejuvenation. . . . Proust's method is actualization, not reflection. He is filled with the insight that none of us has time to live the true dramas of the life that we are destined for. This is what ages us – this and nothing else. The wrinkles and creases in our faces are the registration of the great passions, vices, insights that called on us; but we, the masters, were not home. [I 344–345/SW2:1, 244–245]

We are growing old in Benjamin's world rather than Proust's. Proust's involuntary memory is elusive and fragile, and may not save or redeem a life as it seems to promise to. But while it lasts it restores the world, the fading world is not consumed in a lightning flash. Proust writes of 'happiness', and of 'a joy akin to certainty' [Recherche IV, 446/Search VI, 176]. The consumed world and the lightning belong to the scenario of Benjamin's rigorous melancholy. We might say he believes in loss even more than Proust does.

In a famous section of *Berlin Childhood* Benjamin revises Proust quite openly, although without mentioning him at all. The section concerns *das bucklichte Männlein*, the little hunchback, a figure once well known to German children, and whose canonical appearance is in the collection of folk songs and poems called *Des Knaben Wunderhorn*, brought together by Arnim and Brentano.

Benjamin recounts his memories of gazing into underground rooms through gratings on the city street, and the reversal of this gaze in his dreams, where creatures from the rooms are looking at him, gnomes in pointed hats. He recognizes the kinship of these figures with the little man, and he quotes a stanza from the poem:

When I go down to my cellar stores
To draw a little wine,
I find a little hunchback there
Has snatched away my stein. [K 78/SW3, 385]

The gnomes and the hunchback are at home in cellars, they are the mischief-makers of folklore. They cause trouble just for fun but they terrify the young Benjamin. As a child he didn't understand them and he didn't know what to call the hunchback; 'only today' has he recognized the name because he remembers that whenever he fell down or broke something, his mother would say, 'Greetings from Mr Clumsy' [K 78/SW3, 385]. *Ungeschickt*: the little man is clumsiness itself, one's own clumsiness showing up as a person. In such moments, Benjamin now thinks, the little man must have been looking at him, because whomever he looks at fails to pay attention. A failure of attention, in this idiom, could run from clumsiness to neglect.

Wherever the little man appeared, Benjamin says, 'I had aftersight', something like an afterthought in the realm of vision: belated sight perhaps. Howard Eiland imaginatively translates the phrase (*hatte ich das Nachsehn*) as 'I could only look on uselessly' [K 79/SW3, 385]. *Nachsehen* can also mean regret or guilt, something like clinging to the idea of a fault. But the context suggests rather a failure of memory to be true to the perceptions of a former time. Things withdraw themselves from this form of sight, shrink in it, become dwarf versions of themselves. The little man appeared to the child Benjamin everywhere, kept getting in the way. Yet he did no harm, only introduced 'the half part of oblivion' into everything the child touched or approached.

'I never saw him', Benjamin says of the little man. 'It was he who always saw me' [K 79/SW3, 385].

If the little man is a manifestation of what we break or forget through inattention, then the contamination of aftersight, which is the little man's contribution to the aging process, the withdrawal or shrinking of things in the memory, is also a failure of attention – as if attention, or a sufficient quantity of attention, might have been able keep them the right size. The little man is a figure for distraction, and he is harmless – but so are small losses, until we add them up. There is no involuntary memory here to restore things to their own old dimensions.

The little man, we might say, is one more obstacle that stands between Proust and Benjamin, however close they may be in other respects. The little man is distraction in the form of the enemy, a long way from the friendly habits of the moviegoer. But then Benjamin goes a step further than Proust. For Benjamin memory resurrects not only what forgetting has preserved for us – Proust writes of a memory which, 'thanks to forgetting' makes such surprising connections [*Recherche II*, 4/Search II, 222] – but provides a set of 'images that we had never seen before we remembered them'.[40] Before we saw them, that is, in a form that felt like a memory to us. Rebecca Comay says this process 'inaugurates repetition as the return of that which strictly speaking never happened', and goes on to make a brilliant link to Benjamin's history essay: 'it announces the redemption of a failed revolutionary opportunity at the moment of most pressing danger'.[41]

For Benjamin realities are literally born in memory, because in memory we can look at what wasn't looked at in the present. The phrasing is not easy, and I translate Robert Kahn's translation from the manuscript: 'There we are facing ourselves as we certainly have been in the most distant past, but never under our own gaze'.[42] This is a beautiful reversal of the little man story. He looked at the child all the more sharply when the child failed to look at himself. Now the grown child, the adult, is able to be present to his own unshrunken past, and memory at last becomes a refutation of forgetting, not a Penelope work at all, but a new tapestry that calls for no unraveling. As Carolin Duttlinger points out, 'the hunchback emerges as an agent not of forgetting but of recollection, as his distracting presence enables these childhood scenes to be preserved, and subsequently remembered, with hallucinating vividness'.[43] At the end of distraction, it seems, lies not concentration but sheer, new immediacy.

In one of the notes for his essay 'On the Concept of History', Benjamin strikingly inverts an image of Marx's. What if revolutions are not the locomotives of history but instances of the passengers reaching for the emergency brake? For Benjamin even Marx was too dedicated to a progressive, linear view of history, not interested enough in distraction, and those passengers are responding to what Benjamin calls in the essay 'a moment of danger' the moment in which, with any luck, the past will flash up to help us. He doesn't mention Proust in the essay, but we recognize involuntary memory in its ambitious new political guise, and in case we don't, we find the connection in Benjamin's notes: 'The dialectical image can be defined as the involuntary memory of redeemed humanity'.[44]

Here are the two crucial sentences:

> Articulating the past historically does not mean recognizing it "the way it really was." It means appropriating a memory as it flashes up in a moment of danger. [I 253/SW4, 391]

Of course the involuntary memory becomes a little less involuntary in its alternative career. It was no part of Proust's thought that one could appropriate such a memory, still less have power over it. Benjamin insists that 'there is nothing inevitable about the dependence on chance in this matter' and rather wishfully finds in Proust a possibility that 'voluntary and involuntary memory may cease to be mutually exclusive' [I 188, 189/SW4, 315, 316]. These claims are true in several important ways of Proust's practice, but couldn't be further from his theory and from the large-scale myths about memory and the will he wants his work to orchestrate.

'There is a great deal of chance in all this', Proust writes [*Recherche I*, 43/Search I, 47]. There is only chance. It's true that Proust romanticizes the difficulty, embraces it, and Benjamin hopes it will go away, but structurally Benjamin's political translation remains loyal to Proust's apolitical theory. Even if we can make ourselves masters of the memory when it flashes up, we can only hope that the flash will occur when the danger arrives.

III

You will have noticed that distraction keeps disappearing from its own history, or at least fleeing to the margins. Ruskin was interested in the undetected influence of art rather than the eye that didn't see it, and the period Mao invokes was absorbed by the thought of the experience it couldn't or didn't register, not the failure of the registry. Similarly Proust celebrated moments of rescued time, not the absence of conscious attention that permitted the rescue. And Benjamin's reading of Proust, and his attempted departure from the master's perspective, concentrate on the visitors we missed, 'the great passions, vices and insights that called on us', rather than the curious trick we have of not being at home when in all literal and ordinary senses of the phrase we are there.

But then if distraction receives only a minor role in its own history, it also plays a similar role in several other histories, and such a versatile performer is surely worth watching. The period Mao identifies is home to a whole set of tales of cultural change, and distraction appears in some form in almost all of them. The form of the tale is curiously unchanging – curiously because the tales are all about change – and is well expressed in the refrain of Bob Dylan's 'Ballad of a Thin Man', where something is happening, but a certain Mr Jones doesn't know what it is.

Something is happening – to reason, to time, to the novel, to the human subject, to the idea of experience, to the belief in progress, and to knowledge itself – and we don't know what it is. If we manage to find out, it's too late, as with Proust's narrator and the gesticulating trees, and the Henry James who discovered in 1914 'what the treacherous years were all the while really making for and meaning'.[45] More often, we don't find out, and the more we try the less we learn. 'We knowers are unknown to ourselves,' Nietzsche said, announcing one of our tales (about knowledge) and moving instantly into two others (about experience and time). 'And as for so-called 'experiences', who among is serious enough for them? Or has time enough?'[46] Benjamin himself became a sort of expert on 'experience and poverty' – the title of a 1933 essay – and the invasion of the world by mere information.

These tales are fascinating, and attending to any one of them would be enough to distract us from distraction for a long time. Not least among the grounds of their fascination is the fact that they *are all tales*, that we choose to express our confusion as a narrative, rather than the result or object of an analysis, and as if it was just happening to us rather than our doing anything to set it in motion. But my suggestion for the moment is simply this: if we understood our habits of distraction a little better we would know more about what is happening to us.

PART TWO

Into Practice

But why are we moderns so distracted?

J. W. von Goethe, *Italian Journey*

FOUR

Kinds of Cool

I

If you play jazz alone, it isn't quite jazz. We find no exact equivalent for this restriction in classical music. There is plenty of ensemble playing, and many solos require accompaniment. But a Beethoven piano sonata, whoever plays it, is as complete as a Beethoven symphony. By contrast, Oscar Peterson is the Oscar Peterson Trio, Dave Brubeck is the Dave Brubeck Quartet, Miles Davis is the Miles Davis Quintet, or Sextet, or the amazing Nonet that resulted in the album called *The Birth of the Cool*.

There are exceptions, of course: the piano work of the incomparable Lennie Tristano or certain tracks and concerts by Keith Jarrett. But they feel like exceptions. When we say the name Bill Evans we hear piano, bass and drums, we add the musical voices of Scott LaFaro and Paul Motian. When we hear the lonely sound of Miles Davis' trumpet, we wait for the quite different assertions and inventions of John Coltrane or Cannonball Adderley.

A good test of this feeling – this sense that in jazz we are almost always hearing more or other or absent music – is the arrhythmic introduction to any number of pieces, followed by the arrival of the percussion and the beat. In Mary Lou Williams' version of 'Autumn Leaves' (1979), for example, there is a full minute of solo piano presenting the whole tune, all 32 bars, with lots of flourishes and vaguely classical pauses. Because the work is played so often, we are ready for some soft brush-work on drums to come next, and a romantic mood, something slinky and Parisian in accordance with the song's origin. Instead, as soon as the minute is over, piano and percussion hit a driving, up-tempo rhythm, much closer to bebop than to late-night smooching. This doesn't stop Williams from playing the tune beautifully and rather slowly over this energetic base, and the lyricism is still there. But it's not what we expected. I'm not suggesting that jazz arrives with the beat, or that jazz itself is all rhythm; only that the rhythm transforms the introduction, just as the introduction sets up the surprise of the rhythm. As the performance continues, we are still hearing what we heard at the start. When we play it again, we are waiting for rhythm before it comes.

Yet another test of our hearing what is not there is the frequency with which, listening to a jazz version of a popular song, we find the absent words, or some of them, running in our heads. I don't actually miss the words as I listen to Coltrane playing 'Every Time We Say Goodbye', and I don't supply the whole lyric. But the phrases 'die a little' and 'how strange the change/from major to minor' do seem to inhabit the wordless sounds, and even create a form of counterpoint. Coltrane's grieving tone is so firm and unhesitant, so authoritative, that if anyone is going to die in his work he or she will die a lot.

We meet a related version of this test in the way in which wind instruments in particular invite us to reach for metaphors of human speech and singing. 'People tell me my sound is like a human voice and that's how I want it to be', Miles Davis said. 'The hardest tune I ever had to play in my life was 'I Loves You, Porgy', because I had to make the trumpet sound and phrase like a human voice'.[47] It's important to understand what this claim means for the music. Davis is not trying to turn his trumpet into something else, or suggesting we would do better to listen to a recording of the opera *Porgy and Bess*. He wants his instrument to say what words can't say, and metaphorically it does, again and again. But then he knows too, as a practitioner, that trumpets don't literally say or sing anything. That is part of their virtue.

A good final example of this alternative or multiplied hearing is the litter of musical quotations that mark so many jazz performances, quick glances at another tune, another time and place and tone, only audible if we know the reference and like this kind of wit. They don't change the individual act, and it doesn't matter if we don't hear them. But they salute memories, they call up company, they say that this music is not alone. We listen perhaps to Miles Davis' version of 'Some Day My Prince Will Come'. A single note is repeated on the bass, accompanied by drums, the piano spreads out a few chords, all this in waltz time – not unheard of jazz, but pretty rare even so – and then the tune appears on the trumpet, broken, beautiful, tragic as it never was in its source, Walt Disney's *Snow White* (1937). It's not just that a piece of sentimental America has become cool beyond belief, and that an old optimism has turned to near despair – no prince will ever come in this rendition – it's that the very sorrow inhabiting this performance, the world of pain it evokes, is the song's new meaning, a belated patch of the blues discovered in the musical mainstream.

I want to suggest that only some form of distracted listening can begin to do justice to these moving and complicated occasions. We don't need to learn how to do this, it's what we do already when we listen to jazz. But if we want to think a little more about what's happening, we shall need to examine our distracted examination,

A plausible starting point is the jazz club, full of smoke (in the old days), conversation and clinking glasses. There is a real resemblance here to Benjamin's cinema. Both places are full of other people and not all are watching the movie or listening to the music. But the club and the cinema, at this stage of history, are more like mythological homes of particular art forms than points of origin for what is actually going on. We can concentrate on a jazz performance amid the smoke and noise just as well as in a concert hall – better, probably, for a host of reasons.

But the myth helps. The club doesn't exist only for the music, and the scene of distraction reminds us of the way the music makes use of distraction on its own terms, the sense it conveys of being rich and present and also haunted, full of absences we can almost hear.

II

We glimpse something like a small cultural revolution in the title and notes of Miles Davis' album *Birth of the Cool* (performances recorded 1949–1950, collection released as an album 1957). The time is a little late for the birth, and Pete Welding's intelligent liner notes resist the idea anyway:

> Let's reaffirm something: catchy album title notwithstanding, the music of the Miles Davis Nonet was, is anything but cool. Controlled, lucid, tightly focused, succinct – yes. It's all of these and more, but cool in the sense of being dispassionate or otherwise lacking in the funda-mental emotional characters one always associates with the best jazz, no![48]

The *Merriam-Webster Dictionary*'s account of the 1950s meaning of the word 'cool' feels rather helpless. The term 'dispassionate' appears. 'Cool', we are told, can mean 'excellent' or 'all right' ('That was a really cool movie'; 'Is getting together Friday night cool with you?'). These easy synonyms miss much of the work the word is doing, and one idiomatic American example seems distinctly off: 'We used to fight, but we're cool now'. Surely the sentence doesn't simply mean the contestants have calmed down.

By contrast, and perhaps surprisingly, the *Oxford English Dictionary* has all kinds of information for us. It has older examples which point to the newer usage: 'cool insolence' in an 18th century adaptation of Shakespeare; 'a right cool fish' in the work of a 19th century British journalist; 'as cool as you please' in a novel by Sherwood Anderson. We learn that the *Bridgeport Telegram* proclaimed in 1948, 'Hot jazz is dead. Long live cool jazz!' A jazz historian, Leonard Feather, wrote in 1955 of an 'understated, behind-the-beat style', associating it with Miles Davis.

To be cool is not to be unstressed but to look and sound as if you don't know what stress is. Of the music of *Kind of Blue* Richard Williams says 'Not only did it not care if you didn't like it, it affected not to notice'.[49] He also associates the word with French and Italian films of the early 1960s. A 'really cool movie' is not just 'excellent', in fact, it wouldn't have to be that good a movie at all. It would have only to feel indirect, unwilling to underline what it was up to. The coolness of insolence, of a person or a gesture is not, in the OED's older cases, necessarily a merit, but a certain admiration lurks in the concept. And cool jazz is not the opposite of hot.

We experience this discretion, this freedom, when we listen to certain tracks of the after all aptly named *Birth of the Cool*. I am thinking especially of 'Jeru', 'Boplicity', and 'Moon Dreams', and it is not an accident that Gerry Mulligan wrote the first of those numbers, and plays on every track of the album. It is all Miles Davis' work in so many ways, but Mulligan sets the tone. It's as if he can't be ruffled. As if.

The ensemble ought to sound heavy – it includes two saxophones, a trombone, a French horn and a tuba, apart from piano, bass and drums and Davis' trumpet – but it doesn't; only densely textured. 'Jeru' and 'Boplicity' are 'cool' in the sense of not making any fuss while delivering a rather intricate musical message or perhaps posing a quiet riddle: how can so many people sound as if they are so few? Or to shift to another figurative register: how can this innovative band make us feel so much at home, as if we have been hearing its style for ever?

'Moon Dreams' is cool in another way. The tempo is slow, and the sound of a set of lower-pitched instruments in unison creates an effect that would be threatening if it were not so gentle – well, perhaps is a little threatening anyway. Against this background, dreamy saxophone solos by Lee Konitz (alto) and Mulligan (baritone), introduce an atmosphere of reflection, suggesting we should always find time to let our minds wander a little, whatever menace may be in the air, and Davis' trumpet floats above the whole affair as if quietly on guard. 'Cool' here means stylish and almost at ease on the edge of darkness.

III

Kind of Blue was recorded in New York in two sessions that took place in March and April 1959. The original album had five tracks: 'So What', 'Freddie Freeloader', 'Blue in Green' (recorded in the first session); 'All Blues', 'Flamenco Sketches' (recorded in the second). The band is composed of Miles Davis, John Coltrane, Paul Chambers, Jimmy Cobb. Bill Evans plays on all but one track, where he is replaced by Wynton Kelly; and Cannonball Adderley also sits one track out.

The album is clearly the sort of work that needs quite a bit of *studium* before we are likely to encounter anything interesting by way of a *punctum*. We have plenty of good material to help us here, almost too much in fact – we could easily be distracted from our distraction. There are three books devoted solely to *Kind of Blue*, major passages in many others, and it appears everywhere in jazz history and jazz legend as the most famous and most successful jazz album ever made. Some cognoscenti prefer the album *Milestones* (1958) because it is more fiery and closer to the blues – for them the 'kind of' in the title of the later work means 'not quite enough'. But everyone acknowledges the musical breakthrough of the 1959 sessions, and there has been much discussion of Davis' turn to a new 'tonal path' based on modes rather than chord sequences.

The question here for me – the point of distraction theory as I am trying to unfold it – concerns what even the more generous types of concentration may miss if they can't relax. I have four areas I'd like briefly to explore: the differences and similarities between the sounds and styles of Davis and Coltrane; the relation between titles and music on this album; the actual effect, as distinct from the formal properties, of the modal method; and the role of Bill Evans in this company, an artist who seems much closer to Maurice Ravel than to Charlie Parker.

The differences between Davis and Coltrane – even if their work together created 'the greatest jazz collaboration ever', according to the subtitle of Griffin and Washington's book[50] – are easy to plot in biography, character, looks, attitudes. The just-mentioned volume has a fine description of a famous photograph taken in a recording studio:

> Miles stands behind a hanging microphone, muted horn pointing down into the mike. He is in a characteristic Miles stance, graceful, poised, weight on right leg, left hip slightly tilted . . . Behind him stands Trane. The most obvious thing about him is the horn positioned horizontally across his waist. He stands solidly on both feet, grounded to the floor; there is no dancer's grace, but a determination that anchors him there . . . Miles is the sure one, the center of attention . . . Trane, even when he is not playing, seems too focused on the music to be concerned about much else.[51]

We have to allow for the fact that if Trane was playing his solo, many things about the picture would be different. Still, the main suggestions of style would remain intact. A great performance of the song I have already mentioned, 'Every Time We Say Goodbye', was filmed in Berlin and as his solo ends, we see Coltrane look down at his instrument and nod slightly, as if to say, in slight surprise, 'We did it again, didn't we?' Miles is the sure one, and Coltrane is lost in the music.

But when we listen to them, as distinct from watching them or thinking about them, the stories are precisely reversed. Davis' trumpet is lost and haunted, Coltrane's sax is striding and confident. The effect is especially clear on the first two tracks of *Kind of Blue*, 'So What' and 'Freddie Freeloader'. On the first, Davis' solo is spare, almost awkward, leaving plenty of space, reaching for bent, broken sounds; then Coltrane sweeps in, full of musical authority, playing lots of notes, seeming to move faster although the tempo is the same. On the second, Davis gets the same effect of frugality, and seems to be squeezing sounds out of a trumpet that would rather be doing something else; Coltrane enters like a new chief executive, the man who has been hired to get this song into proper shape, cure it of its hesitations.

We hear the same Coltrane sound on the fourth track, 'All Blues', and find ourselves charmed and baffled again by an effect that can place a man so totally in charge and allow him to be so completely undomineering. But then on the other tracks, 'Blue in Green' and 'Flamenco Sketches', something else seems to have happened, and we are struck by how alike Davis and Coltrane are after all, how close they can sound; how confident Davis' sorrow can be, how diffidence can creep into Coltrane's ease. Is it because these tunes produce a more subdued Coltrane, or bring him more fully into Davis' orbit? This could be a musical version of the question Griffin and Washington ask and answer about the personal relations of the men to each other. Were they 'two musical geniuses battling it out night after night'? No, because 'Trane was too humble, and Miles, quite simply, was too cool'.[52]

The real question then for the distracted examiner, already sagging a little under the weight of the apparent contradictions, is what we have gained when we recognize the reversible stories of life and music, and learn to hear something of the elements of each that hide in the other. Davis and Coltrane are different and the same: an affair of contrasting effects and secret affinities. That's true, but too easy; too obvious, as Barthes would say. We need to register more trouble and more difficulty, and this is where I would like to return to my earlier thought of hearing what is not there. Listening again and again to *Kind of Blue* I find myself attending more than ever to the music of Coltrane's silence as Davis plays, and vice versa. The result is not harmony or resolution, a settling of what might be a quarrel between doubt and assertion, but rather a faint, searching uncertainty, an awareness of what the other story might mean for the story playing right now. Eric Nisenson suggests that 'there is an edge of suppressed joy in this music'.[53] Joy is going a bit far, even if suppressed. But there is authority in Davis' introspection, and there is introspection in Coltrane's authority. The elements don't combine but each quietly lingers, to borrow a metaphor from Barthes, at the party the other is throwing.

There is a similar dialogue, or at least a similar tug of sounds and meanings, in the relations between the music and the titles on the album.

Does 'All Blues' as a track contrast with the 'kind of' in the album's name, and will the music tell us? If the track title is ironic, a glance at the doctrine that says jazz is blues or nothing, how does the irony work? What do we make of 'Blue in Green'? The sensible (sensitive) reading – a touch of sorrow in the midst of fresh or innocent things – is too tame, and in any case the tune doesn't sound anything like that in this performance.

Let's address these puzzles by listening a little more closely to 'So What', where some beginnings of answers show up more clearly. The musical form here follows the call and response pattern of gospel hymns – Davis said the album as a whole was influenced by the church sounds he heard as a child walking 'the dark roads of Arkansas'.[54] The bass makes the call and the ensemble replies with a two-note phrase that would structurally be an amen. The sequence runs with variations through the whole piece. The trouble, or the interest, lies in the fact that 'amen' is emphatically *not* among the meanings of 'so what'; and 'so what' is definitely what the music is saying. Or 'saying'.

It's hard to be strict or literal about the verbal or mental meanings of music, but some of them do impose or exclude themselves pretty firmly. Proust's character Charles Swann is deeply puzzled by the thought that one could trace a composer's mental illness in the music itself, but he doesn't think it's impossible. On the next track of *Kind of Blue*, 'Freddie Freeloader', named for a character Davis knew who liked to get into shows without paying, there is a two note statement similar to the one on 'So What', but no one would think this is what it is saying. 'There-there' would be more appropriate, or 'O-kay'. This is a twelve-bar blues in form but relaxed and chirpy in tone. 'So What' is also a blues but sounds sceptical even about suffering. I find myself imagining a church where the congregation keeps saying 'so what', and perhaps we don't need to be told that the phrase was one of Davis' favorites.

As for the modal method, I had always assumed that the number 'Flamenco Sketches' was an early gesture towards Davis' album *Sketches of Sp*ain but Richard Williams proposes a quite different sequence. The modal form lends 'an unmistakable Moorish accent to each individual improvisation', which 'may have inspired Davis's title'.[55] I pause over this suggestion because of an effect in the piece that has always seemed curious to me, and curiously beautiful. As I hear it Davis' solo sounds 'Moorish' from the start, since it hovers around a single note as flamenco singers do, creating an extended tremolo. This may well be a direct expression of the world of the title, in which case a piece of Williams' proposition would fall away. But then the other solos, by Coltrane, Adderley and Evans, don't sound 'Moorish' in this or any other sense – until they reach their Phrygian mode. (The modes are Ionian, Dorian, Phrygian, Lydian, Mixolydian, Aeolian and Locrian) Then they each sound as if they were imitating a muezzin calling to prayer.

Williams' proposition is persuasive and attractive, and I hesitate to accept it only because I can't quite believe a mode has such a specific local effect and I can't quite hear it taking place. But I don't have a better theory, and perhaps the chords of the new mode, discreetly supplied by Evans each time, themselves have an Orientalizing flavor, enough to trigger a similar response in his companions. The rest would be cultural memory making music – a way of saying perhaps that there were blues before the blues.

In the end, I take 'kind of blue' to be a genuine variety and not a dilution of a mood, not a synonym for 'blueish'. It is a cool kind, though, it doesn't advertise misery, and certainly doesn't compensate by clowning. This is what Davis thought other trumpeters like Gillespie and Armstrong did, for example: 'I always hated the way they used to laugh and grin for the audiences'. 'I ain't never been no grinner', Davis says[56] – one of the more lavish understatements we are likely to meet. Griffin and Washington aptly (and bravely) translate Davis' manner as saying, 'The coon show is officially over; we are here to play'.[57] Of course Gillespie and Armstrong weren't part of any such show either, and Davis didn't think they were. He thought the impression might arise, though, and the relation of blues to black history is simple in one sense and complicated in another.

Ralph Ellison says the blues reflect 'an impulse to keep the painful details and episodes of a brutal experience alive in one's aching consciousness',[58] and it is certainly true that without the weight of black experience in America, and the complicity of white privilege and prejudice, the blues would not have been born. But there are many ways of keeping history alive, and especially in music, where pain can only appear as madness does in the music of Proust's imaginary composer Vinteuil: transmuted, made up of notes and chords and inflections alone.

A racial theory of this situation – where the ache does not cross a colour-line – might seem to be confirmed by the presence of the Jamaican Wynton Kelly on the 'Freddie Freeloader' track, and the markedly more bluesy sound of the solo. The white man Bill Evans, the pianist on all the other tracks, does not sound like that. What's more, I think we have to say that whatever part of Evan's melancholy comes from history, that history has to be different from the one I have evoked, and perhaps not brutal at all. But then the bravery of the blues, the sorrow that is never only sorrow, can migrate into different forms of music and consciousness, and that, presumably, is why Davis could both think of the roads of Arkansas and invite Evans, who had left the band some months earlier, to rejoin the group specifically for these two sessions.

In this sense 'kind of blue' becomes a manifesto rather than a bit of modesty: this music is bluer than anyone knew music could be, or blue in ways we hadn't thought of. This is just what we hear on the amazing track 'Blue in Green'. It opens with a piano statement of strange, falling chords, their implied tune picked up immediately by the muted trumpet, which then rises to a haunting sequence of high notes, where the sound itself seems on the point of splitting. A short, dreaming piano solo comes next, followed by Coltrane's improvisation, disciplined, quiet, lonely. Then the piano returns, maps out a series of chords, to be followed by a magnificent trumpet solo whose notes keep almost dying, as if Davis has gone astray somewhere inside a musical mood – but not really astray, we know he can still see the path from where he is. The track ends with piano chords and bowed bass, bringing us calmly back from what have felt like perilous places.

If Davis and Coltrane are the lingering guests at each other's parties, Evans is something like the host's indispensable sidekick. In this sense the dispute about who wrote 'Blue in Green' is instructive for us, however annoying it was to the contenders. 'All compositions are by Miles Davis', the record sleeve says. Evans remembers that one day Davis

> wrote on some manuscript paper the symbols for G-minor and A-augmented. And he said, 'What would you do with that? ' I didn't really know, but I went home and wrote 'Blue in Green'.[59]

Davis says 'the first time Bill saw any of that music was when I gave him a sketch to look at just like every one else'.[60] This is a reference to the legendary start of the sessions where Davis arrived with five sketches, and everyone got to work.

Both men can't be right about the first sight of the sketch, of course, but they both have to be right about almost everything else. There is no contradiction, for example, between Davis' sketching the tune and Evans' writing it. *Kind of Blue* is the creation of Miles Davis because he knew the sort of sound he wanted. But he knew also that he needed Evans to get it. The overall sound could include Wynton Kelly's bouncier manner but it was going to be determined by Evans' intricate, inward moods, a curious match to Davis' own, in spite of all the differences. They both have the reputation of being gloomy fellows but a wonderful anecdote about them suggests something else, an ability to make and take jokes, a way of getting earnestness to unwind. It involves an extraordinary, gender-marked riff on the racial question. When Evans joined the otherwise all-black male band, Davis explained that it was part of the group's ritual that a new member had to sleep with each of the others. Evans thought carefully about this and then said that he just couldn't do it. Davis beamed – a smile much wider than a grin, no doubt – and said 'My man'.[61]

IV

We can be distracted examiners of classical music too, but we have to choose to be, to cultivate the paradox of a willed relaxation of attention. I want to think of Richard Strauss' *Four Last Songs* in this context, and to concentrate – or fail to concentrate – on the last of them and its magnificent, Beckettian attempt not to end. The songs were composed in 1948, and premiered in London in 1950. Kirsten Flagstad was the soloist; the Philharmonia Orchestra was conducted by Wilhelm Furtwängler. Strauss died in the intervening year.

The first three of the *Last Songs* are settings of poems by Herman Hesse, called respectively 'Spring', 'September' and 'Going to Sleep'. The fourth song is called 'At Sunset', literally 'In the Red of the Evening' (*Im Abendrot*), and is based on a poem by Joseph von Eichendorff. The text is spoken/sung by someone who says 'we', recounting a life's journey – 'Through sorrow and joy/we have walked hand in hand' – and reminding a partner that it will soon be time to sleep. 'How weary we are of wandering', the voice says'. 'Is this perhaps death?'

Wie sind wir wandermüde –
Ist dies etwa der Tod?

Weary of wandering is a good translation, but the German, literally 'wander-weary' or 'travel-tired', offers a larger array of suggestions. We may be tired by traveling as well as of traveling, we could be tired of the very idea of travel, or travel could have its own quite specific form of fatigue. *Wandern* is obviously cognate with wandering, but also means journeying, going places, or just hiking, and *auswandern* means to go into exile.

The slight word *etwa* may be the most interesting and freighted term in the poem. It does mean 'perhaps', and that is the usual translation in this context. But it also means 'approximately', 'in some respects' or 'are you really suggesting something like this?' Eichendorff's line is sometimes translated as 'Can this be death?' And *etwa* may be just an expletive (*Merriam-Webster*: 'a syllable, word, or phrase inserted to fill a vacancy . . . without adding to the sense'). We see at once how poignant the usage becomes in the poem and the song. When you know you are about to die, why are you saying perhaps, or even offering the most extremely diluted form of the notion? I'm not sure I would ask this question of the poem alone – Strauss's setting has done a great deal for it, and in any case it was through the setting that I arrived at the poem.

The *Last Songs* were associated for a long time with Elizabeth Schwarzkopf, who made many recordings of them in the 1960s. In 1982, Jessye Norman created a now classic version – the orchestra was that of the Gewandhaus, Leipzig, and the conductor was Kurt Masur. I'm thinking mainly of this performance, but, as you will see, I have Schwartzkopf in mind too. It is significant for my purposes that the Norman version of 'Im Abendrot' is the slowest: it takes nearly ten minutes compared with Schwartzkopf's just over eight, and the seven minutes of many other renderings.

The last of the *Last Songs* opens with a long, sumptuous orchestral sequence stating the theme of the piece, just short of two minutes for twenty-two bars, so we are not surprised that when the voice ceases – I will not say dies – there is plenty of lovely, swooping sound to come. Even so, for a work about ending, it seems to be taking an inordinate amount of time – over two and a half minutes in fact, so that the symphonic opening and closing sections occupy almost half the piece.

When the voice reaches *Wie sind wir wandermüde*, the notes drop down the scale, as if sinking, as if there were nowhere else to go. There is a slight delay before *wandermüde*, which arrives on the second beat of the bar – perhaps the word was not quite ready or not quite right. But then the notes rise cautiously with the question of the last line, and the word 'death' hangs on a marvelously unresolved chord. The voice ends its sentence trying not to know the answer, perhaps. In Schwartzkopf's version there is, however faintly sketched, more resistance, more denial. The question is a kind of protest – surely this can't be death?

The orchestra has been murmuring its richly textured notes between the sung words – between *dies* and *etwa*, and between *etwa* and *der* – as if it were eager to take over, or perhaps feels the voice is failing and needs help. It does take over in any case, and introduces a new question. We know that death ends life, but do we know how a masterpiece ends when it doesn't want to end? Like this, Strauss says. In the silence of the voice, the orchestra recapitulates the end of the last stanza, we hear again the falling tune of the confession of weariness, then a sequence of chords, tentatively rising and falling, groping for something. The orchestra arrives at what seems to be its last full chord and then starts upwards for another one, only to return the previous chord and move up again. The larks from an earlier stanza, represented by flutes in the orchestration, reappear as if nothing had happened, and no one was tired, and the hesitation continues. The piece closes in a place that is entirely conventional musically, the major chord of the key of the whole work, but this home doesn't feel like home, and Strauss emphasizes this feeling by having the larks twitter twice more, and by offering the same chord one more time, an end beyond the end.

I'm afraid this all may sound like too close listening rather than any sort of reception in distraction. But then I am trying to suggest that close listening – or close reading or close viewing – may be an exercise in distraction, or at least relatable to that habit, as long as we overdo it. There is a real link here to D. A. Miller's marvelous concept (and practice) of 'too-closeness'.[62] Miller suggests that Alfred Hitchcock in his films is playing a game 'with that absurdly, pointlessly watchful spectator who dwells within us all, but whom, as members of a mass audience, or as critics in loyal alignment with it, we mostly put on lockdown'.[63] This figure, Miller goes on to say, can't quite be the Roland Barthes of *Camera Lucida*, because Barthes' *punctum* is private, and the instances seen in a film by the too-close viewer are indisputably there for everyone. Hitchcock 'defies [us] to continue overlooking them'.[64] The question is not about the objective presence of this or that extraneous image (face, book, painting) but about what we are supposed to do with it. It has no narrative or interpretative function, but we can't, once we have registered it, make it disappear. It is 'latent if you don't see it, overwhelming if you do'.[65] And here is where obsessed concentration and thoroughly indulged distraction may join forces: neither of them will leave the field to the well-informed, disciplined observer, the old-fashioned correct examiner. In this sense even close reading as we have been practicing it in literary criticism for so many years may have had its own form of remoteness, a certain tendency to self-policing: we took care not to get too close.

I should stress also that I have been talking about Richard Strauss and not another composer. If you want to write music that lets go, as Strauss did in his later life, you have to subvert a whole classical discipline, so I would need to start again in order to show what a distracted examination of the *Goldberg Variations* might look like. That's a good idea, especially since Glenn Gould made his first recording of them in the same studio that saw the birth of *Kind of Blue*, so let me . . . No, another time.

In the following passage, Edward Said is thinking mainly of Strauss' *Metamorphoses*, but the *Last Songs* are not far away. Strauss' late work, Said says,

> is, I believe, radically, beautifully elaborative, music whose pleasures and discoveries are premised upon letting go, upon not asserting a central authorizing identity, upon enlarging the community of hearers and players beyond the time taken, beyond the extremely concentrated duration provided by the performance occasion. In this perspective afforded by such a work as *Metamorphosen*, music thus becomes an art not primarily or exclusively about authorial power and social authority, but a mode for thinking through or thinking with the integral variety of human cultural practices, generously, non-coercively, and, yes, in a utopian cast, if by utopian we mean worldly, possible, attainable, knowable.[66]

That's not what we mean by utopian, but it's a generous gamble to believe that we might or could. If we can't take distraction seriously, we can't imagine these freedoms. Beyond concentration and time taken lies a world of new habits.

FIVE

All That Dread

I

I want to write about W. B. Yeats' poem 'Lapis Lazuli' in the context of distraction because I have long been interested in its style and modes of argument, and have also long felt that its central proposition is unpersuasive, even unpleasant. Does the concept of gaiety do the work it is supposed to do, and what happens if it doesn't? Could the word have interesting effects in spite of itself, or in spite of what Yeats wants to do? Much depends on how we feel about Nietzschean gaiety, but perhaps even there an intended claim and an achieved result are two different things.

It is hard to think of Nietzsche as a distraction from reading Yeats. The influence is glaring, and happily confessed: 'that strong enchanter' was what Yeats called him.[67] 'Bitter and gay' were words Yeats liked to join up, although he borrowed them initially from Ernest Dowson rather than Nietzsche. But then Nietzsche himself wanted to be a distraction from almost everything, and one could surely go too far even in the right direction. This chapter is an attempt at a close reading of a poem and also at something more obtuse in Barthes' sense, a reading that finds its way into distraction and doesn't entirely leave it. I realize that every distraction runs the risk of becoming too relevant, but I am taking Barthes' wry claim as a sort of wager: 'If I deliberately strove for the effect of disorder, I would produce only a *stupid* disorder' [OCIII, 1031/RF 193, Barthes' italics]. If I don't try too hard perhaps I can get disorder to do a little useful work.

The central difficulty that besets 'Lapis Lazuli' is even clearer in 'The Gyres', the work that precedes it in Yeats' *New Poems* (1938). The unmistakable success of this piece, as so often in Yeats, lies in its eloquent failure to mean what it says.

Irrational streams of blood are staining earth;
Empedocles has thrown all things about;

Hector is dead and there's a light in Troy;
We that look on but laugh in tragic joy.

What matter though numb nightmare ride on top,
And blood and mire the sensitive body stain? [CP 293]

By the end of this brief poem (24 lines), Yeats has asked 'What matter?' four times, proof enough perhaps that his answers are not working. The light in Troy doesn't shine for the defeated Trojans, and 'tragic joy' is a phrase, a gesture, a wish, not a condition of mind that Yeats can get himself, let alone us, to believe in.

We know from a 1935 letter to Dorothy Wellesley the mood he was seeking to evoke: 'the lasting expression of our time is . . . a sense of something steel-like and cold within the will, something passionate and cold';[68] and we recognize in the last three words an inversion of a phrase from the poem 'The Fisherman', where the titular figure ('A man who does not exist,/ A man who is but a dream') is a person for whom Yeats will one day 'have written . . . one/poem maybe as cold/And passionate as the dawn' [CP 149]. This freezing passion is a long way from tragic joy, though, even if the joy and the coldness are equally remote from any felt reality. In 'The Gyres' nothing matters more, it seems, than the irrational streams of blood and the numb nightmare. In 'Lapis Lazuli', however, Yeats comes much nearer to success on his own declared terms, which is where my problem with this magnificent poem begins.

The work is dedicated to Harry Clifton, the man who gave Yeats the small Chinese carving he transports in imagination into the world of the work, and this is where the gaiety finally, insistently resides. We may start by noting the interesting rhymes for the key word in its adjectival form: say, play, day, play. And then we might – or is this a distraction, in which case we must – want to think of some of Yeats' uses of the word in other poems. They are relaxed at times – so relaxed we could think the hysterical women of the poem's first line were right, at least about this poet – but sudden and troubling at other moments. The word can be contrasted with 'dull' or 'solemn' or 'sad', or paired with 'terrible'. For example:

The waves were more gay,
When I was a boy with never a crack in my heart. [CP 21]

Gay bells or sad, they bring you memories
Of half-forgotten innocent old places. [CP 45]

'This is not' I say
'The dead Ireland of my youth, but an Ireland
The poets have imagined, terrible and gay'. [CP 320]

Never to have lived is best, ancient writers say;
Never to have drawn the breath of life, never to have looked into
    the eye of day;
The second best's a gay goodnight and quickly turn away. [CP 227]

The last quotation is from Yeats' version of *Oedipus at Colonus*. There is
something wonderfully Edwardian about the gay goodnight, and I'm
not quite sure how to characterize another fine touch in that work,
Yeats' description of Dionysus as 'Semele's lad' and 'a gay companion'
[CP 218]. For the record I should say that other translations speak of
the god's revels and dancing, but none that I know of calls him a lad.
I think of Housman's *A Shropshire Lad* but also of the old idiom 'a bit
of a lad'.

II

One of Nietzsche's major works is called *The Gay Science* – the English
title is actually closer than Nietzsche's own (*Die Fröhliche Wissenschaft*)
to the form of the 'gaya scienza' that he was interested in. This was an
old Provencal concept that expressed the 'unity of singer, knight and
free spirit' represented by the troubadour [GS, note on title page].
Nietzsche's work is both essayistic and aphoristic and is framed by two
sets of poems. The tone is well set by a brief dialogue between two
speakers simply named A and B:

B: But why, then, do you write?
A: Well, my friend, I say this in confidence: until now I have found no other
    means of getting rid of my thoughts.
B: And why do you want to get rid of them?
A: Why do I want to? Do I want to? I have to.
B: Enough! Enough'. [FW 108/GS 91]

Writers are garrulous, Nietzsche says. 'There is a garrulousness of rage – frequent in Luther, also in Schopenhauer'. In Kant we find 'an exceedingly large supply of conceptual formations', in Montaigne 'a delight in ever-new twists of the same thing', in Goethe 'a delight in good words and forms of language', in Carlyle 'an inner pleasure in noise and confusion of feelings'. There is also 'a garrulousness of spiteful natures' – Nietzsche doesn't give instances but says 'whoever reads the publications of our time will recall two writers here' [FW 111/GS 93]. And Nietzsche himself? What makes him talk so much? Because he has to get rid of his thoughts. By why does he have to? And if he had different thoughts would the situation be different? By 'writers', we note, he means in this context mainly but not exclusively philosophers.

A crucial aspect of gaiety for Nietzsche is that it is not opposed to thought or seriousness. It might be the mark, for those who can achieve it, of the only true seriousness. 'For most people', he says, 'the intellect is an awkward, gloomy, creaking machine that is hard to start. . . . The lovely human beast seems to lose its good mood when it thinks well; it becomes "serious"'. 'That is the prejudice of this serious beast against all "gay science"'. Nietzsche sees only one option: 'Well then, let us prove it a prejudice!' [FW 202/GS 182–183] Not an easy task, and Nietzsche himself is not exempt from the serious beast's distrust. How could he understand it so well if he was? At the end of the last but one prose section of the book he announces a 'great seriousness': 'the real question mark is posed for the first time . . . the destiny of the soul changes; the hand of the clock moves forward; the tragedy begins' [FW 281/GS 247]. Then he realizes he has lost sight of the gaiety he has been preaching – in any case, how could one preach gaiety? – and thinks he hears laughter all around him: 'most malicious, cheerful, hobgoblinlike laughter: the spirits of my book are themselves descending on me, pulling my ears and calling me to order [FW 281/GS 247].

Does everything look like a parody of itself, are these the last days of the old world? The spirits are ready: 'Was there ever a better hour to be gay?' [FW 281/GS 248, translation slightly modified]. It's a wonderful invitation, but even here Nietzsche hears a call 'to order': the old Protestant in him never quite lets go. Perhaps only an old Protestant could be quite so keen on a theory of gaiety. The mood came more naturally to Semele's lad, and of course Nietzsche was one of the lad's great admirers.

I suspect others may hear as I do, in that creaking machine and the prejudice of the serious beast, an anticipatory echo of the day of 'theory' in literary study. We were too serious about it, we didn't know we were allowed to enjoy it. Paul de Man said

> There is something bleakly abstract and ugly about literary theory that cannot be entirely blamed on the perversity of its practitioners. Most of us feel internally divided between the compulsion to theorize about literature and a much more attractive, spontaneous encounter with literary works.[69]

With friends like these . . .

This is where the deep attraction of Nietzsche's thinking lies. It is always about knowledge as an adventure and a pleasure, about theory as a thing of beauty. We should be laughing not at what we know but at the act of knowing. 'Life could be an experiment for the knowledge-seeker – not a duty, not a disaster, not a deception!' '"Life as a means to knowledge" – with this principle in one's heart one can not only live bravely but also live gaily and laugh gaily' [FW 200/GS 181]. Even if we cannot entirely manage to achieve this life and laughter, as Nietzsche certainly could not, we shall be better off for having a feeling for what they might mean. He wants us to make ourselves 'braver, more persevering, simpler, more full of gaiety' [FW 215/GS 193].

This is the implication of Nietzsche's claim that 'perhaps even laughter still has a future'. If we understand the 'ultimate liberation and irresponsibility' of thinking about the species rather than the individual then 'perhaps laughter will then have formed an alliance with wisdom; perhaps only "gay science" will remain' [FW 36/GS 27–28]. Of course species-thinking is not all it takes, but I would argue that a mixture of laughter and wisdom wouldn't be bad for the individual either. The enemy for Nietzsche is our caution and common sense, our idea of balance and propriety.

> And ever again the human race will from time to time decree: 'There is something one is absolutely forbidden to laugh at'. And the most cautious friend of man will add: 'Not only laughter and gay wisdom but also the tragic, with all its sublime unreason, belongs to the means and necessities of the preservation of the species'. 'And therefore! Therefore! Therefore! Oh, do you understand me, my brothers?' [FW 38/GS 29]

A good answer might be 'not quite', since the cautious friend is also Nietzsche, wearing another hat. He does believe that gay wisdom includes the tragic, but does not, at this moment, want to give the binary see-saw any space. Therefore? We should find a new consequence for a new situation. Or perhaps throw all 'therefores' away. Nietzsche's aphorisms can be seen as a profligate set of instances of what it means to do without neat logical deductions. Such sayings are an aspect of the practice of what he calls 'looking away', *wegsehen* [FW 171/GS 157], a combination of distraction and willed blindness that allows him, as Rei Terada has eloquently shown, to pursue his persistent feeling that 'there is something wrong with dissatisfaction with reality'.[70]

This perspective is important because for Nietzsche much of what we call knowledge is merely a tired recital of what we think we know. This includes science in all its senses, and more specially our adages and received ideas. The scientists and philosophers are attacked first because they are a supposed avant-garde of thought dedicated to rearguard reactions. 'How little these men of knowledge demand', he says, or more loosely, 'How pleased with themselves these knowledgeable people are!' He wants us to understand the practice of knowing as a more dynamic affair. 'To know' could mean 'to view as a problem, to see as strange, as distant, as "outside us"' [FW 240/GS 214–215]. This is not too difficult in relation to the natural sciences: 'they take the strange as their object'. But then there are what Nietzsche brilliantly calls 'the unnatural sciences', which seek to explore the familiar. We might now call them 'the humanities', as Bernard Williams suggests [GS x], although in so saying we would lose some of the mischief of Nietzsche's thought. Certainly the 'science' of his title allows for any form of organized knowledge, but he wants us to see how weird the adventure of knowing can be – especially when it concerns what we think we know. 'What is familiar is known', he says, as if inventing a proverb, more literally 'What is known is known' – he uses two different but closely related German words: *bekannt, erkannt* [FW 240/GS 214–215]. The proposition is entirely wrong, Nietzsche says.

> The familiar is what we are used to, and what we are used to is the most difficult to know [*Das Bekannte ist das Gewohnte; und das Gewohnte ist am schwersten zu "erkennen"*] . . . it is nearly contradictory and absurd even to want to take the not-strange as one's object. [FW 240/GS 215]

Of course we do know the familiar – that is one of the working meanings of the word knowledge – but not in the way Nietzsche is seeking to recommend. Even if we don't lazily or fearfully convert the unknown into the known, that is, ignore the unknown entirely, we do usually regard knowledge, in its active sense, as a foray into strangeness. And if we choose to explore the not-strange, as happily we also do, we usually make it strange first. Then we can set about knowing it. This is how Victor Shklovsky's critical practice works. Brecht's alienation effect too. Roland Barthes's mythologies are written in this mode. It's also very often the goal of close reading. We can only be grateful for practices that serve us so well, and hope for more of them. But could we also do what Nietzsche asks of us? Explore the not-strange in its not-strangeness?

We could think of Samuel Beckett's whole work as devoted to this project. There are disciplines driven by this kind of exploration: psychoanalysis, some forms of philosophy, represented for example by Wittgenstein's interest in optical tricks and children's puzzles. We pursue it in ordinary life when we think about the jokes we laugh at, or pause over stereotypes or clichés. But how often do we make it a function of literary criticism, theory or scholarship? If we did, would we still be laughing? Is there a way in which we could, to borrow Nietzsche's marvelous phrase, 'become bright again' [FW 275/GS 243]?

III

This would be the moment to think about some of the resonances of the English word 'gay' and Nietzsche's 'fröhlich'. 'No one, presumably', Bernard Williams says, 'is going to be misled by the more recent associations of the word "gay"' [GS x]. This is surely right, and the German word has none of these associations anyway. But both words have a certain affinity with trouble – more precisely enact a kind of denial of the trouble they are apt to court – and this affinity makes them available for certain games with usage. Think of Yeats' characterization of Dionysus as 'a gay companion' and his image of the 'gay goodnight' of despair. Williams himself says Nietzsche's 'gaiety' is an expression of 'daring, individuality and creative bloody-mindedness' [GS xiv], which are perhaps not the qualities we most immediately think of as gay. 'Bloody-mindedness' is almost Freudian in its accidental reach. Williams' implication is clearly that of his English idiom: awkward, unwilling to give up. Obtuse, we might say. Webster tells us the usage is 'chiefly British', and means 'stubbornly contrary or obstructive: cantankerous.'. But Webster's first meaning is 'inclined towards violence or bloodshed', and this is, wouldn't you know, among Nietzsche's specified implications for gaiety: 'who would know how to laugh and live well who did not first have a good understanding of war and victory?' [FW 200/GS 181] In a similar . . . er . . . vein Nietzsche offers a wonderful revision of Hobbes' definition of laughter as 'nothing else but sudden glory arising from some sudden conception of some eminency in ourselves by comparison with the infirmity of others or with our own formerly'.[71] 'Eminency' is perfect, both lofty and abstract, and miming exactly the self-satisfaction in the thought. Nietzsche's version is: 'Laughter means: to gloat, but with a good conscience' [FW 161/GS 141]. 'Gloat' translates *schadenfroh sein*, to be happy about damage or distress. We see the *froh* that is at the heart of *fröhlich* and cognate with the *Freude* that goes into the English word *Schadenfreude*.

IV

We don't have to think this is all laughter is, or this is the only kind of laughter, in order to accept the uncomfortable truth in these claims, and with this we can turn back (at last) to the Yeats poem, which half-wishes to keep these connotations at bay. We read that 'Hamlet and Lear are gay'; that 'old civilisations' are 'put to the sword'; that a pair of ancient Chinamen, with glittering eyes, are also gay [CP 294]. It's hard to avoid the feeling that Shakespeare's tragic characters are gay because they know they can't die, like mere non-fictional humans; and that the builders of new civilisations must be very close indeed to the mood of sudden glory, of good conscience, when they think of the broken and vanished worlds that came before them. There is a delicate evasion in Yeats' wording which allows him to skirt this issue.

The old civilisations are 'built again', as if they came back from the dead, as if they had the option of not perishing before the new civilisations rise. The finality of the falling is masked by the idea of return. I suppose if we stand far enough away the old and new civilisations may look the same, but then this grand sort of distance, if inhabited too eagerly, makes the poem simply heartless. The Chinamen are a different matter, and the whole poem leads to them.

Let's go back to the beginning, and move slowly.

I have heard that hysterical women say
They are sick of the palette and fiddle-bow,
Of poets that are always gay,
For everybody knows or else should know
That if nothing drastic is done
Aeroplane and Zeppelin will come out.
Pitch like King Billy bomb-balls in
Until the town lie beaten flat. [CP 294]

The poet doesn't say he has heard the hysterical women, only that he has heard of them, been told what they are saying. Why this indirection, is he really claiming not to have heard such stuff himself? And who says the women are hysterical, is this the poet's epithet, chosen on the basis of their reported talk, or is it the word his informant used? Either way it is, in this male-centred time and context, almost a tautology. It was once supposed that hysteria could arise only in women, hence the popular assumption that if they are women, they'll be hysterical, and if they're hysterical, they'll probably be women. We meet the same adjective-noun conjunction in Fitzgerald's *This Side of Paradise* ('I can imagine the stream of hysterical women fluttering at your doors')[72] and indeed in *The Gay Science*, although Nietzsche, rather surprisingly given his usual view of things, includes both sexes in the purview: 'we know these hysterical little men and women' [FW 274/GS 242], the sort of people who engage in 'the religion of compassion'.

Here's a truly distracting thought. Was Yeats thinking, should we think, of the women in Eliot's 'Prufrock' as they 'come and go,/ Talking of Michelangelo' (twice)?[73] 'Probably not', is the answer to the first part of the question. 'Why not, if we feel like it?' might serve as a response to the second. Yeats had certainly read the poem when he made his selection of seven poems by Eliot for his *Oxford Book of Modern Verse*, even if he didn't include it. But I have other associations here. Christopher Ricks, in a brilliant chapter of his book on Eliot and prejudice, says readers are right to pick up 'a whiff of the prejudicial' in the lines, an implied comment on the women. But critics are 'wrong to write as if what were before them were not an impalpable smell but a palpable dossier', and still more wrong to 'write a novel' instead of reading the poem.[74] If they were reading carefully they would notice the absence of any adjective where we have seen 'hysterical'. Well, of course they do notice on one level, that is why they have to slip their qualifiers in. One critic says the women are talking 'no doubt tediously and ignorantly', another hears 'some contempt' for them in the line. Yet another thinks the voices must be 'high-pitched' and another says the women are 'trivial'.[75] Given this pile-up of unquestioning interpolation Eliot's silence becomes striking: 'the women'. As Ricks says, it's not that the readings are necessarily wrong, although they are flat-footed by any standard. It's that they have read a silence as a form of flag, and this is why I think of Yeats' hysterical women in this context – in one draft he called them 'some queer women'.[76] They are hysterical (or queer) because they are ready-made, and for the same reasons that their relatives in 'Prufrock' are tedious, ignorant, contemptible, squeaky and trivial. They are a social fantasy. A male fantasy, of course, but also a fantasy entertained by the supposedly cultured whatever their sex, an assumption about all those who do not know what we know. Yeats' trick is to catch this fantasy on the wing, make it talk, and then borrow its language for another use.

We understand the shrill – another adjective-in-waiting – error the women are making but we are about to learn that they have the right word nevertheless, the key word. It's what they are sick of. Their complaint is quite subtly graded. They disapprove of the current state of the arts, but make distinctions. At first there is painting itself, presumably of any kind (the palette), then frivolous-seeming music (represented by the fiddle-bow, not even the fiddle itself, which does however evoke popular Irish music as well as Nero's famous performance while Rome burned), and then a quite specific allegation about poets: they are always gay. Always, even in times of crisis. They don't know what 'everybody . . . should know'. At this point the poet starts parodying the women rather than just quoting them. What are they thinking? Do we expect poets to do 'drastic' things even if they are appropriately serious? When did a poet last prevent a war? And should the war be prevented if it means joining forces with Hitler, King Billy's current avatar, as the Irish fascists whom Yeats admired wanted to do?

The vagueness of the hoped-for action matches the vagueness of the threat, and here the parody gets really complicated, mocking the idea of crisis even as it asserts it. There will be no Zeppelins in 1936, and if King Billy is the German Kaiser Bill, he belongs to an older war. If he is the Dutch-English William III, as he certainly also is, he has been dead for more than two hundred years. Scholars tell us that the poet has taken both the name and the oddly-identified 'bomb-balls' from an old Irish ballad about the Battle of the Boyne (1690):

King James he pitched his tents between
The lines for to retire;
But King William threw his bomb-balls in,
And set them all on fire. [CP 506]

The poet seems to want to defy the women by proving them right. He gaily turns the threat of war into a recurring violent farce. But then he can't quite keep up the tone. 'Until the town lie beaten flat': where is the gaiety there? This is the impossible question the poem sets out to answer. The town, we might note, is far more local than any of the centres of civilisation that appear later in the poem. It's a place where people live. The word has a glow of sociability, as in 'about town', 'on the town'. It's where women and poets reside, where the lads and lasses go out to play. Or will until they are bombed.

V

All perform their tragic play,
There struts Hamlet, there is Lear,
That's Ophelia, that Cordelia;
Yet they, should the last scene be there,
The great stage curtain about to drop,
If worthy their prominent part in the play,
Do not break up their lines to weep.
They know that Hamlet and Lear are gay;
Gaiety transfiguring all that dread. [CP 294]

There seems to be no antecedent for the word 'all' in the first sentence. It doesn't look as if it could include the women, the painters, musicians and poets of the previous stanza, and still less King Billy, so we must think of it as an announcement rather than a recall. But perhaps we are moving too quickly. Maybe those figures are caught up in the play – because there is no other, and we and they are 'everybody' – and just don't know it. The Shakespearean characters, on the other hand, do know it. They perform, as we all do, but they are artists, they 'do not break up their lines to weep'. Or they break up sometimes, depending on mood of the character or the skills of the actor. The conditional clause introduces a wonderful complexity into the illustrative image here. 'If worthy their prominent part in the play'. It's easy to see how an actor could fail to live up to a role, a little harder to see how a character could be an unworthy instance of the character he or she is. This is the double implication, though, I think, highly concentrated in Yeats' best elliptical fashion. Actors play the parts of Hamlet, Lear, Ophelia and Cordelia, and they don't need to be worthy of any prominence to get through the show, they just need to be competent. Hamlet, Lear, Ophelia and Cordelia, we may say, are also actors, although the parts they aspire to play are their own, sketched by Shakespeare in the script he has written for them. It is possible for them, or for anyone, not to be loyal to their best selves, not to make it to the end of their own play. But here is the most powerful suggestion in this part of the poem. The actors/characters speak their lines all the way through without breaking up not because they are professional or achieve a moral coherence, but because of what they know. They know, actors and characters alike, that tragic heroes are gay. The poet adds a coda to the proposition, grammatically unconnected, as if there were nothing to say about such gaiety except to recall what it does, to mention its task of 'transfiguring all that dread'. There is the word 'all' again, repeating its uncertain inclusion, and we are about to hear it in the next line, calling up 'all men have aimed at, found, and lost'.

All what dread? Well, all that. Whatever dread we found in those two Shakespeare plays, and in the intricate metaphor that has been developed from them. We may need to return to the conditional clause. If the tragic figures did not know their own gaiety, if they were not gay, would they be unworthy of their names and fame? What happens to dread that doesn't get transfigured? The question is the more urgent because several of Yeats' other uses of the word fail vividly to promise much by way of transfiguration:

Dread has followed longing,
And our hearts are torn . . . [CP 263]

I sing what was lost and dread what was won . . . [CP 312]

What need have you to dread
The monstrous crying of wind? [CP 122]

There is a sort of answer to the question, though, in the rest of this part of the poem, even if the sentences are cryptic and incomplete at first:

All men have aimed at, found and lost;
Black out; Heaven blazing into the head:
Tragedy wrought to its uttermost. [CP 294]

Four conditions. No indicative verb animates them or connects them, they simply occupy the space of dread: human aim, black out, blazing Heaven, tragedy. And then we are told something we already know: a play is a play.

Though Hamlet rambles and Lear rages,
And all the drop scenes drop at once
Upon a hundred thousand stages,
It cannot grow by an inch or an ounce. [CP 294]

Ah, but do we know what we know? And have we given any thought to the possibility of a hundred thousand productions of *Hamlet* and/or *King Lear* being put on at once, and therefore ending at (roughly) the same time? The poet has turned time into space, because he knows it's easier to imagine Shakespearean performances across the centuries than to see every one of them as contemporary with all the others. The word 'all' is again doing quite a lot of work. I don't know what a 'drop scene' is, but I can see why the poet wanted to get the word 'drop' twice into one line.

And why is this an answer? I didn't say it was an adequate one, and I want to point to one more word lacking a close referent. What is the 'it' that 'cannot grow by an inch or an ounce'? Grammatically it has to be 'tragedy', but the effect of the sentence is to imply a looser connection. 'It' is also whatever the poem has been talking about: the play, the dread, the aims of men, the black out, the blaze, the rambling and raging, the dropping. And even if 'it' is tragedy it is now singular and generic: not the separate destinies of four characters in two works but 'tragedy wrought to its uttermost'. It's not just that a play is a play. It's that there is only one play. And given the complexion of the play in question, gaiety would be a heroic condition to achieve. That is how I take the apparently confident 'They know that Hamlet and Lear are gay'. They don't know, but it would be wonderful if they did; worth asserting beyond proof or present incarnation.

The syntax is strange again in the way that Yeats' syntax so often is. 'They' are Ophelia and Cordelia, and there is no reason why the women should know of the men's gaiety; no reason either why the characters in one play should know anything at all about the characters in another. No reason, that is, except the vast dream of transfigured dread, which anyone can share, and anyone can fail to have faith in. Certainly gaiety has taken on a deeper, scarier meaning than it had in the poem's third line, and perhaps this is all the poet needs to have done with the notion as yet.

VI

On their own feet they came, or on shipboard,
Camel-back, horse-back, ass-back, mule-back,
Old civilisations put to the sword.
Then they and their wisdom went to rack:
No handiwork of Callimachus
Who handled marble as if it were bronze,
Made draperies that seemed to rise
When sea-wind swept the corner, stands;
His long lamp chimney shaped like the stem
Of a slender palm, stood but a day;
All things fall and are built again
And those that build them again are gay. [CP 294–295]

This stanza, like the previous one, seems to start a new poem. We feel a little lost, seek to build the bridge that isn't there. 'They' must be the people who arrived wherever they were arriving, but subject of the sentence is 'old civilisations', which are 'put to the sword', in poem-time, before they have got anywhere. The next lines tell us about their wisdom and their sculpture and their 'things', but this has all gone 'to rack' as soon as it is named. 'Rack and ruin' is the more usual phrase but the poet leaves the second half to us. And here he performs a bit of his customary magic. Nothing 'stands' but here is a whole Greek civilisation caught in a sculptor's name and a wonderfully evocative set of analogies. Callimachus 'handled marble as if it were bronze,/Made draperies that seemed to rise/When sea-wind swept the corner', and made a 'long lamp chimney shaped like the stem/Of a slender palm'. If this isn't standing, then poetry doesn't exist. The argument recalls that of the opening of 'Nineteen Hundred and Nineteen', with its mention of 'an ancient image' on the Acropolis and 'Phidias' famous ivories'. All gone, but are we surprised?

Man is in love and loves what vanishes,
What more is there to say? [CP 208]

This is a version of 'all things fall', but the poet does now have something more to say: 'All things fall and are built again'. In context, this claim is, excruciatingly, both true and false. All things can be rebuilt in memory, or in a poem. The literal work of Callimachus and Phidias, of a whole Greek civilisation, is gone for ever. It seems almost frivolous, far too 'gay', to conflate the two perspectives. 'Those that build them again are gay' is an astonishingly, willfully blinkered line. Any builders may be gay, and probably should be, but there is no building 'again' here. As I have suggested, the things that fall and the things that rise are far from being the same. It is only in a kind of crossed-consciousness – the kind we saw when Ophelia and Cordelia were said to share the moods of Hamlet and Lear – that a civilisation survives its death, that Greece become Rome. 'Civilisation' is then a concentrated abstraction like 'tragedy'.

Two Chinamen, behind them a third,
Are carved in Lapis Lazuli,
Over them flies a long-legged bird
A symbol of longevity;
The third, doubtless a serving-man,
Carries a musical instrument. [CP 295]

A change of scene: from west to east, but still in the realm of carved materials. Again, the abruptness matters, the blunt annoucement. After the rather too tripping and articulate sentence about falling and building and gaity, we are offered a simple fact: 'Two Chinamen'. We then learn there's a third as well, and we get a verb for the sentence, delayed and emphasized by its place in the new line: 'Are carved'. There is also a carved bird flying, helpfully identified for us as 'a symbol of longevity'. It's hard to think the poet is not smiling when he rhymes this word with 'Lazuli'. He's sure about the details as well as the symbol: the third figure 'carries a musical instrument'. The word 'doubtless' introduces a different note, though, reminds us that a particular mind is looking at a stone, thinking about what it sees, writing what it sees, turning stone into situation. It's a good guess, of

course; but so easy a guess that it scarcely seems worth introducing a
doubt, even to cancel it.

Every discolouration of the stone,
Every accidental crack or dent
Seems a water-course or an avalanche,
Or lofty slope where it still snows
Though doubtless plum or cherry-branch
Sweetens the little half-way house
Those Chinamen climb towards, and I
Delight to imagine them seated there;
There, on the mountain and the sky,
On all the tragic scene they stare.
One asks for mournful melodies;
Accomplished fingers begin to play.
Their eyes mid many wrinkles, their eyes,
Their ancient, glittering eyes, are gay. [CP 295]

This stanza makes clear what the poet is doing, and not only through
the repetition of 'doubtless'. He is reading the stone for what it is,
attending to 'every discolouration . . . every accidental crack or dent',
but also turning these markers into a three-dimensional picture of
something else, not stone at all, but water, snow and hillside. 'Seems'
is his way into this movement, but his second 'doubtless' actually
invents a place that the climbing figures – the figures seen as climbing
– haven't reached yet, and the rest of the poem stays with them in this
place, with the poet frankly declaring his role and his pleasure in all
this: 'and I/Delight to imagine them seated there'. 'There' is a halfway
house with a plum or cherry tree close by, and at first seems to be the
mountain too. But they can't be seated on the sky, and the sly double
use of 'on' changes the perspective. They look up or across at the landscape and down 'on all the tragic scene', ideal spectators of the play we
have so far only thought of through its players.

One of the Chinamen 'asks for mournful melodies' and 'accomplished
fingers begin to play'. We are not told what the instrument is, but we
can assume it is not a fiddle but something like a lute or lyre, and we
may pause over the mournful melodies. Why do they want these, if they
are going to be gay, if they are offered as a final, definitive epitome of
gaiety in the face of tragedy? Everything in these last lines, and indeed
perhaps in the whole poem, depends on timing. Here it is precisely a

matter of how long, and in what fashion, to defer the arrival of the word 'gay'. Just think of the main clause: 'Their eyes are gay'. Then work slowly through the delays: first a detail, many wrinkles; then a repetition of the subject, their eyes; then an adjective, ancient; then another one, glittering; then yet another mention of the eyes. Of course the poet could have gone on longer, but he knows when to stop as well as when to defer, and the triple appearance of the eyes, especially after the fingers in the previous line, makes the Chinamen themselves almost disappear, to be replaced by isolated organs. No humans here, only agents of performance and perception. We can even wonder whether the Chinamen themselves are gay. Perhaps they are sad, teaming up with the music they have chosen. But then the gaiety of their eyes is all the more impressive. The eyes understand the poem they are in, even if none of the humans, factual or fictive, do. They are ancient, and they glitter, and are gay.

The glitter is both appealing and horrible and I find it impossible not to see a touch of malice in that glitter, an element of whatever the Chinese is for *Schadenfreude.* Elsewhere Yeats writes of the 'glittering eyes' of a death's head [CP 186], and even equates glitter with the energies of repression:

. . . the wild thought,
That she denies
And has forgot,
Set all her blood astir
And glittered in her eyes. [CP 140]

He also said that 'the east . . . knows nothing of tragedy. It is we, not the east, that must raise the heroic cry'.[77] In the poem he is permitting himself to get things wrong, allowing the Chinamen actually to see a 'tragic scene' and still remain Chinese. Their gaiety would have a (projected) placidity that westerners cannot know; but they in turn would recognize western dread when they saw it. These magical figures can't feel any malice in their pleasure, so the actual words of the poem play on both sides here. And this, I think, is the secret of its amazing success. It does precisely what Nietzsche couldn't do, it takes the cruelty out of the gay science, but not by denying or even transfiguring the cruelty. It lets the cruelty flicker there, an integral part of a gaiety that is free to laugh at any thing, and will not weep when most people weep, but also does not laugh when the town lies beaten flat.

SIX

Playing the Witch

I

In the course of writing this book, trying to be faithful to old habits of distraction and to pursue new ones, I have watched the ground of the work shift, or rather become a little more diverse. My initial guess was that distraction would contest but not replace concentration; it would no longer simply be opposed to it. Further, although the theory of distraction I was trying to piece together began in the cinema as far as both Benjamin and Barthes were concerned, I thought it unlikely that its interest would be confinable to that medium It wouldn't work for all films, or for films only.

So first, I felt we needed to understand a habit we already possess, albeit in an elusive and unmapped way. As Benjamin said, thinking in advance (in 1929) of his distracted examiner, it would not occur to anyone that Chaplin needed better critics than his actual audience already provided. And second, I thought we could ask what these habits might do for us if we learned to take them to places where they were not supposed to belong.

But then writing the present chapter, I found I was engaged in a third practice, that of responding to a work that actually cries out for distraction. Not only that, I realized that I had begun even earlier, in my remarks on *Finnegans Wake*, a sketch of the challenge such a class might present. In these instances, it seems, the better we are at intelligent, informed interpretation, the worse things get, the more the work slips away from us. We need to learn a new habit of distraction, not only to understand and export the old ones.

Painting and the fine arts in general provide Benjamin with his prime examples of works that need to be concentrated on, that will not tolerate distraction. Distraction and concentration certainly 'form a antithesis' for him, and he illustrates their difference by a quick slide into architecture. 'Architecture has always offered the prototype of an artwork that is received in a state of distraction and through the collective' [I 166/SW4, 268]. He then has a whole paragraph about buildings and the eternal human need for shelter. Next, he collapses buildings back into architecture but invents a new distinction between using such structures and perceiving them, between *Gebrauch* and *Wahrnehmung*. Benjamin's terms make perfect sense to me, as does his notion that 'the concentrated attention of a traveler before a famous building' doesn't begin to come to terms with either architecture or shelter [I 166/SW4, 268]. I think, for instance, of the Camino Real hotel in Mexico City, a 1967 masterwork by the architect Ricardo Legoretta. I've spent quite a bit of time there, and I love its belated Bauhaus feel as well as its spacious, rather austere New World tone. But I don't always think of it as architecture. Sometimes it's just a hotel, a place to stay, great rooms, drinks, crowds of people.

I don't find Benjamin's translation of use and perception into what is 'tactile' and what is 'optical' quite so useful; it seems too neat and mock-technical. Still, an important point swims up through the sense-imagery. The optical is associated with contemplation and attention (*Kontemplation, Aufmerksamkeit*), the tactile with habit (*Gewohnheit*). In fact – here is where the schematic oppositions fold into each other and pay off – with architecture the optical *becomes* the tactile since in this instance both are determined by habit. Architecture is the old training ground that allows us to understand how our new training ground can be the cinema.

> For the tasks which face the human apparatus of perception at historical turning points cannot be performed solely by optical means – that is, by way of contemplation. They are mastered gradually – taking their cue from tactile reception (*Rezeption*) – through habit. [I 166–167/ SW4, 268]

Habit is a good word here, but we need to catch its near-synonyms too: custom, manner, fashion. We might say the German words *Gewohnheit* and *gewöhnen* remember more clearly how habits are formed: through use. And another near-synonym – practice – echoes, as I said earlier, Benjamin's literal term for his training-ground, also translated as a field of exercise: *Übungsinstrument*. There is a slight ambiguity, in German as in English, about the idea of practice, especially since Benjamin says film is the proper or real (*eigentlich*) instrument or field for it. We could practice a skill in the right place, like medicine in a hospital, or we could, as with music in a rehearsal room, practice in one place a skill we plan to use in another.

Benjamin wants to hang on to both meanings, I think, but then we need to watch his sleight of thought carefully. He is using different media to illustrate distinctions in our ways of perceiving, but the distinctions ultimately concern the perceptions rather than the media. In other words, we can look at paintings and architecture as we have been accustomed to look at them, but we can also learn from architecture (and from movies) new ways of looking at paintings. This slippage from art object to the art of interpretation also marks two experiments in thought that are very close to Benjamin in spirit. Jorge Luis Borges' story 'Pierre Menard, Author of the *Quijote*', ostensibly about writing and rewriting, is all about reading and rereading, and the same goes for Barthes' distinction between writerly and readable texts: the writerly is what readers collaborate in and the readerly is what they just consume.

There is still an element of contrariness about a 'casual noticing' [I 166/SW4, 266] of the features of an art form classically constructed by concentration, but this very element allows us, I think, to see something of the urgency of distraction. In the previous chapter I was using a mode of distracted attention – excessive interest in a figure not even mentioned in the poem I was concerned with, fussing at the meanings of particular words beyond any call of close reading – as a way of trying to get at something that has always baffled me about that poem, at my sense that it was some sort of masterpiece and yet apparently had only trivialities to offer us, on the order of 'stuff happens', or 'the play is the thing'. Distraction, I would like to believe, helped us to understand the eerie richness (not complacency) of gaiety and everything associated with it.

II

The painting I want to explore in this chapter, Max Ernst's 'The Witch', seems at first sight to call for nothing but concentrated attention, indeed to exclude everything else. It is so loaded with implications, sexual, personal, alchemical, psycho-analytic, that our likely problem is not bafflement or difficulty, but scholarly triumph. The invited *studium,* we might say, the wealth of opportunities for learned, associative commentary, is so extensive that the *punctum* may not get a look in. This wouldn't necessarily be a bad thing; we don't have to romanticize the *punctum*. But an uninterrupted *studium* does condemn us to meaning, allows for no exemption from the military service of words, and offers no hindrance to critical self-congratulation.

That said, we should probably start with a few studied details. 'The Witch' was painted in 1941, the year in which Ernst left France for the United States. It's a small work (24.5 by 19 centimetres), oil on canvas, and Ernst was using the technique usually called *decalcomanía* because it was adapted for modern use by the Spanish painter Oscar Domínguez and because critics like the sound of mania at the end of the word. A *calcomanía* is a transfer, so the idea involves a dis-transfer or an untrans-ferring. It is a matter of putting together two surfaces (paper, glass, canvas) with wet paint on them, and seeing what images arise. The artist can then turn accident into intention by high-lighting or extending what is hidden or half-hidden in the image. John Russell's description of the effect, published in 1967, is still worth quoting at length. The method is 'ideal', he said,

> for the recreation of substances which are soft, porous, spongey, long-decayed, equivocal and sinister. It is ideal for stone that has been worn to the consistency of old cheese, for vegetation that has been rotting for a hundred years in a swamp, for carcasses in which only bone and horn survive intact, for caverns at low tide, and for architecture that the jungle has had its way with.[78]

We might also think of the room in J. G. Ballard's *The Drowned World,* where 'one of Max Ernst's self-devouring phantasmagoric jungles screamed silently to itself, like the sump of some insane unconscious'.[79] The silent screaming comes from the stories that haunt the images, the narrative turns they suggest. As with much Surrealist work, and espe-cially that of Magritte, Ernst's paintings are full of hints about what happened before and after their particular moments were caught and frozen. Another critic, Uwe M Schneede, says of the results of decalco-manía that 'it is impossible to make out whether a living substance has been petrified or an inanimate one brought to life'.[80]

Paintings by Ernst in this mode, apart from 'The Witch', include 'The Robing of the Bride', 'Napoleon in the Wilderness', 'Europe after the Rain II', and quite a few more. 'The Robing' was painted before he left France. He finished 'Napoleon' in the United States and reworked 'Europe' there. I haven't found a source that gives the exact time of the year for 'The Witch', but I am assuming it belongs to the American half of 1941, since the authoritative *Oeuvre-Katalog* of Ernst's works places it after 'Napoleon' and before 'The Anti-Pope', 1941–1942.

There is a 1939 painting by Leonora Carrington, Ernst's partner at the time, which looks like a prelude to and even a commentary on these slightly later works. It is called 'A Portrait of Max Ernst'. An Ernst lookalike stands in the foreground of a glacial landscape, all ice, snow and water. Just behind him is a large frozen white horse, customarily taken to represent Carrington herself. The Ernst figure is carrying what looks as if it might be a lantern but turns out to be a jar containing a miniature horse, like a sort of incubus. The jar is green and introduces a slight note of colour into the surrounding whiteness. The note is slight, and so is the effect of the darkish brown skin of Ernst's face, since it is topped by hair that is whiter than the ice. What is not slight is the strange dominance of colour in what Ernst is wearing: a yellow sock with black stripes (we see only one of his legs) and an ample, reddish-brown fur coat that extends to the ground and ends in an upturned fish-tail. The work feels like a prelude because of the way the fur coat takes over the picture, and like a commentary because, although the symbolic details belong to a lexicon similar to Ernst's, the style is very different, all clarity and separation, where Ernst's world at this time is amorphous and shifting, 'a world gone soft', as Russell says. To put it too simply, you can't wear a coat or anything else in Ernst's work at this time, you can only grow fur or feathers, start to turn into another creature.

Decalcomanía is the technical basis of a vision. In the Carrington painting the human figure may be standing on compacted snow but the ground is firm and clear. In 'The Witch' and the other Ernst paintings I have mentioned, the very idea of a ground is corrupted, and with it the idea of standing. This is the area where Russell's analogies find their strongest application, in the troubled earth where the figures pose. In the Napoleon picture, the emperor himself looks like a rock formation, and the giant siren who appears not to see him has decalcomanic clothes that are more geological than anything else.

But something else is happening with the witch. As our gaze moves up from the ground the suggestions of stone or vegetation are complicated by other possibilities. She perches awkwardly on a rock that might be a petrified tree trunk, but the lower portion of her clothing, apparently made of exactly the same matter, is clearly some kind of fur growing out of the her flesh rather than just covering it. And what do we make of the same material when it is folded over her (unseen) right arm? Or when it hoods the witch's head, hides her face, and falls elegantly down her back? Now it resembles tree bark with a hint of cloth to it, and its fluid, cascading effect just adds to our bewilderment. We note too that the strange creature standing beside the witch, apparently asking her a question or seeking instructions from her, is made of the same substance as the witch's cloak.

The creature itself, which has two eyes in its head and another, larger eye in its neck, as well as a half-clenched hand that is nearly human, stands more comfortably on the rocks than the witch does, as if it is at home there and she is not. Yet it also represents a taxonomic nightmare. Its hand and wrist extend from what is obviously the sleeve of a removable coat, yet this sleeve belongs to a coat only in another sense, referring to that of a dog or a bear, for example. Nothing else about the creature suggests it is dressed in anything other than its skin.

We need to attend to the non-decalcomanic elements of the painting too, and especially the witch's bare body, the glimpse of a breast, a long, elegant leg, a hip and slender waist seen through the robe that has made itself transparent for these regions. This version of the female nude appears often in Ernst's work of this period, and we are told that the artist was thinking (or wanted us to think) of Lucas Cranach the Younger, and the rather sickly beautiful women he displays in the character of Eve. This is a compelling connection for 'The Robing of the Bride', where the Cranach-style figure appears four times, but is upstaged by an equivalent of the fur coat Ernst is wearing in the Carrington painting. Four versions of Eve, or what a robing of Eve might mean. Or a vision of what happens to the stately forms of Cranach in the busy, self-transforming 20th century.

Benjamin thought Dadaist painting left no room for 'contemplative immersion' because the shock effect was everything. 'The Dadaists turned the artwork into a missile' [I 64/SW4, 267]. This is not quite what happens with memorable Surrealist paintings. The effect is that of a riddle rather than a missile. Another way of saying this would be to say that the best Surrealist paintings have no first meaning in Barthes' sense, no level of straightforward communication or reference. What might have been their first meaning is swallowed up in the second, which is why they seem so crowded with invitations to interpretation. At the same time, interpretation is blocked by all kinds of logical traps. My hope that is a version of Benjamin's distraction, of Barthes' 'erratic and stubborn' attention to a third meaning, will allow us to see more closely how the notion of the impossible plays out in one of these works.

Our uncertainty about the witch's human status – is she part animal and part tree as well? – is complicated by her excessively graceful femininity. How can she be anything other than a woman, or rather a stereotype of an attractive woman? We may think of Cranach and Eve but my first association is with a fashion model or a dancer at the Moulin Rouge. And we can imagine her costume, if it is a costume, as in the process of being removed, a feature of a strip-tease act. This is her witchcraft, a bodily presence, and at this point we may wonder too about the entirely absent trappings and equipment of witchery, the pots, the spells, the newts, the broom, to say nothing of the air and age of the crones who usually play the role.

She does have a version of the witch's favourite companion, though. The yellow creature with three eyes is hardly a cat but it occupies the cat's role. Yet what could such a witch do with such a familiar, and what is it asking, if indeed its gaze and gesture suggest a question? And more urgently perhaps, what do we make of its third eye, which seems to be staring at us while its other eyes are firmly focused on the witch? It's very hard to resist allegory here, to avoid meta-thoughts about eyes and painting. Or eyes and film, if we wish to recall the opening scene of Luis Buñuel's *Chien andalou*. We should recall it perhaps, since Ernst appears as an actor in Buñuel's next film *L'Age d'Or*, and there are many points of resemblance between the preoccupations of the two artists. But let's linger with our first-stage distraction for a while.

The creature presumably, from its point of vision, can see the witch's eyes. But we can't. They are covered by her hair, if that is what is, like the rest of her face except her mouth and chin. We can't learn about her anything of what we imagine we are capable of learning from the look of human eyes. They are not part of her craft, as her breast, waist, buttocks and legs are. The hair in close-up does look like hair, combed forward like an extended fringe, and it may also be hair that falls to the left of her face as we look at it, lining a cloak made of almost the same material. Or we may just be moving back into our taxonomic riddle, and confusing the idea of growth with the idea of clothing.

And here, I think, the question of what we cannot see, intriguing as it may be, is simply swallowed by the visual dominance of what I am calling the cloak, Ernst's version of what he himself is wearing in the Carrington painting. It defines the witch as it hides her, and it occupies a very large proportion of the space within the frame. It shields her head – in one extrapolation of the imagined three-dimensional space of the witch's world it might even prevent the creature from seeing her. It hides both of her arms. It creates a dark space behind her back. It falls almost to the ground, as if ready to embrace the rocks it resembles at that point. It is the witch's darkness, the counterpart to the provocative forward placement of her elegant, bare white leg.

III

Even if it replaces shock with mystery, Surrealism is still often the enemy of habit. But looking at Ernst's witch and her companion, at the rocks on which they stand and the clear blue sky behind them, we can I think usefully call on a habit that is not contrary to the Surrealist program. It depends on a reading of what Benjamin means by the conjunction of distraction and the idea of collective behaviour.

It is dangerous for individuals and groups to claim to know how the masses think and feel. The dictatorship of the proletariat has too often been forestalled by mere dictatorship, or by the rule of a gang that is sure it knows what the proletariat ought to want. But it is possible to find in ourselves those parts of a reaction to a painting or any other work of art that we believe we may share with others, as distinct from the parts that feel private to us. We are inclined to celebrate our more personal reactions, but that's the fantasy of liberal individualism offering a prompt, and when we consider the habits a distracted person may form, I suggest we have to think of habits we may share with others.

In fact, the situation is even more complicated than this, and that is one of the reasons for bringing Benjamin's distraction and Barthes' obtuseness together. At first glance, one writer seems deeply immersed in the idea of a collective mind, while the other seems wildly individualistic. We could think that an interpretation cannot fail to be personal, even if it's not as original as we would like to think; but also that the personal itself is shot through with what we have borrowed from others. Nothing is more common than for a supposedly idiosyncratic view to turn out to be everyone else's view too. Perhaps the best elements of our distraction are not entirely our own.

My interest in 'The Witch', then, lies in what might be obvious in the painting and may feel obtuse. What would we see, for example, if the painting were not called 'The Witch' – or 'The Wizard-Woman', as it sometimes also is? We would (and do) see a young, voluptuous woman half-transformed into an animal, or perhaps caught somewhere between animal and vegetable, between bear or deer and forest. She could be a nymph, or a Surrealist version of something like a female centaur. She seems ready to provoke us in some fashion, but also stands tentatively on the rocks as if she had flown there, and was ready to fly away. Perhaps this is what the creature next to her is asking: Where next? Or is there a doubt in the creature's submissive gaze? Has she declared a plan, and is it asking whether she really wants to go through with it? At this point the possibility that she and the creature may be looking at each other, her glance finding a sideways route through her cloak/hair, seems important because it doubles our exclusion. We can't see her eyes but she can't see us either, doesn't want or need to. Part of her relation to the world is a willed, styled blindness, a coiffure that is a barrier to vision.

What happens when we identify her as a witch – belatedly, as it were, rather than upfront? She is no kind of crone, as I have said, no cousin of the witches visualized by Dürer or Fuseli, or dramatized by Shakespeare and Goethe. She is too elegant for that, and too young; we can't avoid the grace of her bearing and posture. She is not scary, unless we think the ambiguity of her nature is scary enough in itself. But then the title does speak. Once we have heard or it seen it, we can't go on ignoring it. The picture becomes a redefinition of the witch: closer to the beautiful woman as siren, but also, because of her fur, more bestial than her antecedents, farther out from the merely human.

I said her cloak was her darkness, and this is certainly part of the painting's effect: we don't know what magic it might do, or what sort of magic it belongs to. But it is too red and too luxuriant, too similar to Ernst's garb in the Carrington painting, to be only an evocation of darkness. It looks like a form of life, and perhaps signals a transition. Is the witch on her way from being a woman to being an as yet unnameable creature? Will she still be a witch when the transformation is complete? Will she be more of a witch or less of one? I begin to feel the painting is telling me that all women are witches but also that this very proposition is a product of male paranoia or desire, depending on how men imagine they feel about witches. But then the completed transformation would cancel this particular reading, and perhaps the witch's condition in the painting is after all her natural, ambiguous state: she is a witch because she is caught between what is human and what is not.

At this point we may need to look again at her companion, a furry animal with a human hand and a third eye. The creature is not a bird, but there is something birdlike about its face, and it's hard not to think of Ernst's avian alter ego Loplop, who appears in his collage novels as well as his paintings. It's not that the non-bird in 'The Witch' *is* this figure, even in disguise, only that something like a faint memory of the painter and his displacements steals into the frame, as if Loplop himself had avatars that scarcely resembled him. Perhaps the painter sees himself as the witch's too submissive servant, just like the eager, rather worried creature. Since the witch – the figure in this painting, and this vision of what a witch is – is entirely Ernst's creation, he could hardly go further in the denial of what is actually, pictorially happening. Or perhaps the denial is not a denial, but a discreet pointer to the whole fantasy of irresistible charm.

IV

Wouldn't Benjamin say these descriptions and speculations belong to the realm of contemplation and attention rather than that of distraction and casual noticing? He might, but I think the painting itself stands in the way of any steady, coherent interpretation, and Benjamin's distraction seems to be just what we need. Ernst is offering us a riddle rather than a missile, but he is not asking us either to solve it or to muse on it as a mode of enigmatic wisdom. He wants us to be disturbed by it and stay disturbed.

We can think about our disturbance but we can't concentrate on it without turning it into something else. And if we wish to be really obtuse, we can return to the creature's third eye, which looks quite different, and therefore no doubt sees quite differently, from the eyes it directs towards the witch. In fact, the eye looks very much like a lens, photographing our disarray. It doesn't comment, it's a camera, and the creature is busy with something else. Still, I can't help thinking the eye has a question for us, even if it is unlikely that there is a single answer. The question has many contexts, and the eye of Ernst's creature is far from alone in asking it. It is, 'What are you doing here, hanging around, distractedly considering this painting (this poem, this tune, this film). Don't you know how closely you resemble the guest at Roland Barthes' party, the person who doesn't say anything and isn't needed?'

SEVEN

Let's Not Overthink This

I

In their biography, Howard Eiland and Michael Jennings say 'we know relatively little about Benjamin's visits to the cinema other than that they were frequent'. We also know that he was happy about his 'acquaintance with the work of Katharine Hepburn'.[81] It would be good to know more, but this slender knowledge is helpful, since it tends to confirm what we may already suspect: that when Benjamin says 'film', and 'cinema' he is speaking as a moviegoer rather than a cinephile, thinking of a popular art form rather than the avant-garde edges of a newish medium. There would thus be a 'natural', lived context for his theory of reception in distraction, and there would be other sorts of cinema where intense concentration might apply, where 'contemplation' is distinctly appropriate.

I want to close this chapter with a return to a 1970s version of that 'natural' old context. It has changed quite a lot since Benjamin's time but not enough to put the distracted examiner out of business. Before I go there, though, I want to test in another region the pieces of theory I am drawing from Benjamin and Barthes. This would be the place in the cinema where, as with literature, classical music and painting, concentration is supposed to reign and we might want to give it a break. The film I want to fail to contemplate is Luis Buñuel's late work *The Phantom of Liberty* (1974). I chose it because it is a difficult, contradictory film, hard to think of in circulation beyond the art house, and because it is, in my view, an extraordinary masterpiece. I didn't always think this, and I recently found an old note in which I complained of the work's 'dogged arbitrariness', its dedication to 'surrealism in slow motion'. Later viewings made the film seem lighter to me, faster, less programmatic, and that, I think, was because I understood better the necessary collapse of Buñuel's ostensible programme.

The Phantom of Liberty does not cry out for distraction, as *Finnegans Wake* and much Surrealist art does. However, it does mime and examine distraction. All its characters are absent from their own life. The proliferating loose ends in the plot ruin whatever attempts at concentration they make. Yet in the end no one is distracted enough, and the film itself isn't distracted at all. Distraction is a phantom – like liberty itself, Buñuel would say. This is why I think a touch of our second type of distraction, the habit we are not supposed to have in these contexts, may help us to see around it.

The film's title, Bunuel writes in his autobiography, is a 'discreet' reference to the opening of the *Communist Manifesto* ('A spectre is haunting Europe') and it has a mock-theological history within Buñuel's own work. 'Your liberty is but a phantom' is what a Jansenist says to a Jesuit In *The Milky Way* (1969). Through the early scenes of *The Phantom of Liberty,* the title clearly refers to political and social aspirations old and new. But then, Buñuel suggests, it takes on 'another meaning', that of 'the liberty of the artist and the creator, just as illusory as the other'.[82]

Another meaning. Like Barthes, Buñuel is an enemy of all meaning – of what Barthes called the military service of sense or the fascism of words, as well as the discreet charm of imagining we know what is going on – but he is more pessimistic. He sees that even the idea of escaping from meaning is freighted with unshakable significance. The escape is itself an aspect of prison life.

'Bunuel despairs for us', Joan Mellen says, 'doubting not so much the possibility of redemption as its likelihood'.[83] He thinks we prefer our cages to any liberty we might theoretically have. And the images of the film itself certainly won't show us any sort of way out, rather the reverse. But they might, in the form and tone of their arrangement, show us that cages are not everything. And distraction, if it were not a phantom, might hint at a few of the attainable forms of freedom.

II

The dominant trope of *The Phantom of Liberty* is that of a freedom we can't want. When Napoleon liberated Spain from the rule of the Bourbons many Spaniards preferred old domestic oppression to foreign new ideas – the Napoleonic story was very different in Italy and elsewhere – and a famous paradoxical cry arose: *Vivan las cadenas*, long live our chains.

The film opens with a full screen reproduction of Goya's 'Tres de Mayo', a famous painting of an execution during this war. We hear gunshots, and a title card tells us we are in Toledo in 1808 – not Madrid, the location in the painting, but still a scene from the same French invasion. A firing squad marches into a courtyard, and rather motley group of Spanish prisoners shuffles into the frame, noisily dragging their chains – the actors are the producer of the film, Serge Silberman, the poet José Bergamín, a doctor-friend of Buñuel's called José Luis Barros, and Buñuel himself, impersonating a monk. As the firing squad takes aim, Barros steps forward and gives the cry, dropping the d for what was apparently the colloquial pronunciation: *Vivan las caenas*. A sub-title translates the phrase (rather freely) into French: *A bas la liberté*. The film frame now offers a close (but not exact) replica of the painting. We hear the shots but don't see the killing, and another group of prisoners is brought to the wall.

The focus moves to the French soldiers, and their drunken post-execution party. They are doing their drinking in a church. One of their officers decides he would like to kiss the statue of a woman, elegantly praying beside the statue of her husband. The stone husband doesn't like this, and hits the officer on the head, injuring him badly. Some time later, the angry officer raises the lid of the woman's tomb, and finds in it a radiant corpse, dead certainly, but untouched by any of the ordinary visual effects of death or age. As these images fill the screen we hear a woman's voice pronouncing sentences as from a book, and realize that what we have seen, or some of what we have seen, is the incarnation of what for the reader is only text. The story, 'El Beso', by Gustavo Adolfo Becquer, has already been acknowledged in the credits, and it is set in Toledo, unlike the Goya painting. Now we see the woman sitting in a park. She reads 'The implacable hand of death had respected her face, which retained the freshness and the fragile appearance of a rose. . . .'

The film doesn't literally or visually return to 1808 or to Spain, but in one sense it never leaves the atmosphere it has established here, and items of imaginative furniture keep coming back. There are shootings: a sniper fires from a high window in the Tour Montparnasse in Paris, killing several people in the streets. There is another coffin with a female corpse bearing an unusual relation to time and mortality – she makes a phone call to her brother offering to reveal to him 'the true mystery of death'. A reproduction of the Goya painting appears on the wall of a police commissioner's office.

And the theme of liberty receives a parodic twist – as if its first, historical iteration were not parodic enough before the movie got to it. Students – we are in the early 1970s, so the Paris excitements of May 1968 are not far away – are trying to liberate the animals in the zoo at Vincennes. The police are worried, but seem to have things under control. We see shots of various creatures – a rhinoceros, a seal, a hippopotamus, a hawk, a bear, a lion – and we hear all the growls and bleats and squeaks we associate with a zoo. We also hear human shouts and machine-gun fire, and in a wonderful slippage into a world of association rather than mimesis, we hear footsteps and the sound of dragging chains, and a voice cries out, twice, *Vivan las caenas*. The phrase is again translated on a title card (but appears only once) as *A bas la liberté*. There are more sounds of gunfire, and some miscellaneous shouting but we see only two police commissioners calmly smoking their cigarettes. As the noises increase the camera pans very fast around the zoo – too fast for us to see anything but a blur – and comes to rest on the head and neck of an ostrich. We get several different shots of the bird, each one emphasizing more and more its huge and bewildered eyes. Would it cry out in favour of chains if it could? Does its agitated look represent a version of that cry? And what voices, young or old, free or captive, belonging to human or to other animals, might join the chorus? Credits scroll up the screen, and we may note (the published screenplay reminds us if we don't) that the word 'Fin' does not appear.

The film is full of instances of what we might call inferential disorder. The sniper, for example, is tried, found guilty and sentenced to death – the trial, we learn, has lasted fourteen months. As soon as the sentence is pronounced, the condemned man is set free, shakes hands with everyone, lights a cigarette, gives a few autographs, and leaves the court.

A little girl is reported missing from school. The parents rush to the place, talk to the headmistress, are taken to the girl's classroom. The girl, Aliette, is there and everyone can see her. But the evidence of anyone's eyes is irrelevant because the official report of her being missing cancels all other claims, including Aliette's assertion of her own presence. In one magnificent moment a policeman about to set off in search of Aliette asks if he can take her with him to help identify the missing girl. His boss rather sternly says of course not, as if the idea were hopelessly improper rather than nonsensical.

Buñuel repeatedly said he was interested in chance, and of course one can imitate chance, as many great novels and films do. But the imitations are not themselves the work of chance, and so must come close to a betrayal of their own interest. From old Toledo, a scene that turns out to have been a text, we pass to the reader in present-day Paris. She and a fellow nanny are with two little girls who are playing in a park. A wonderfully creepy child fancier gives one of the girls a set of (presumably obscene) postcards, which she takes home. We cut to an apartment where a stylish, gloomy-looking fellow called Foucauld, played by Jean-Claude Brialy (by this time recognizable as a New Wave icon from films by Chabrol, Godard, Rivette and Truffaut), offers what is either the movie's motto or a parody of the same: *J'en ai marre de la symmétrie*, 'I am fed up with symmetry'. His wife is Monica Vitti, an icon from another movie world. She and their daughter now appear, and we recognize the girl who was given the postcards. She hands them over. The parents look at them together and are shocked (and excited). And then we get to see the lascivious images: banal shots of the Invalides, the Madeleine, the Arc de Triomphe, the Eiffel Tower, and finally the Sacré-Coeur. The last is too much for Foucauld, who tears it up, saying *Ça non, tout de même*. A little later he hands the cards back to his daughter as if there was nothing wrong with them. However, he fires the nanny for her negligence in allowing the girl to be approached in the park.

There is a night scene where Foucauld sees various apparitions: a cock striding through the room, a woman carrying a candle, a postman who brings a letter to him, and an ostrich which seems to have escaped not only from local captivity but from the later scene I described above. The next day he consults his doctor, who is dismissive of these visions until Foucauld shows him the material letter the nocturnal postman left. And then the film makes the first of the moves that will characterize the rest of the work: it abandons the Foucauld story and picks up another narrative thread.

This belongs to the doctor's nurse who needs to take a few days off because her father is ill. The film tracks her now, driving to the countryside, staying at an inn. The episode involves monks both praying and playing cards, a flamenco dancer practicing in her room, a hatmaker from Nîmes who hopes, with his scary female partner, to involve the brothers in a bit of sado-masochism, and a young man planning to sleep with his aunt – a person whose naked body, finally revealed, denies the time her face records.

I won't describe each episode in detail, but it is worth noting the breaks, the places where one story is abandoned and another begins. When she leaves the inn, the nurse offers a lift to a professor who is about to give a lecture to a police academy in Argenton, and the film now follows him. After his lecture (with inserted examples), a couple of policemen take off for a bit of traffic duty, and we go with them. Until they stop a man for speeding, that is, and his story becomes our next interest. Like Foucauld, he consults his doctor, and we may be slightly alarmed at this echo – is the film running out of situations? There is an extraordinary moment of grim comedy here. The doctor (called Pasolini) tells the man he would like a to make a small investigative incision. 'Simple medical curiosity', he says. Nothing serious, any time will do. Then he says, 'Will tomorrow suit you?' Scarcely has the man got home with his worries than the phone rings to announce that his daughter is missing from school, and we follow the first part of that story through. It is interrupted by the tale of the sniper, and by the time we return to see the little girl acknowledged as present, the police commissioners have doubled – that is, two different characters (and actors) occupy the same office and have the same secretary. It's the first one who receives the phone call from the cemetery, and is arrested for trying to break into a coffin. Then without any explanation he is back in his office and both police commissioners go to the zoo in the same car. The end of the film is as I have described it.

Maurice Drouzy, in an excellent chapter on *The Phantom of Liberty*, suggests that Buñuel, in spite of his own wishes, 'does not manage to shake off his work habits and his architect's reflexes. He too remains the victim of the rules of symmetry'. Drouzy is thinking of the larger structures of the film and draws up an elegant diagram on the basis of the sequence I have evoked. It begins and ends with what he calls 'repression and gun fire', centres on the episode of the young man and his aunt, and has in each half (in the first and second parts of the film) a church/cemetery scene, a couple with a daughter, a visit to a doctor and a police/army patrol on country roads. For reasons I don't understand, Drouzy places the story with the child fancier, whom he calls *l'homme-satyre*, in parallel with that of the sniper.[84]

My own old take on the film was something like the mirror of this picture. I was concentrating on the sequence and its breaks, but I also felt a project of asymmetry was finally in the business of doing itself in. What we both missed, I believe, was the playfulness of Buñuel's despair, his willingness to juggle rather than resolve contradictions. When he says the liberty of the artist is illusory, he doesn't mean the artist cannot do what he or she wants. He means doing what we want is not a form of freedom unless other conditions are fulfilled, including the condition of actually wanting the freedom we say we desire. In order to get a real feeling for this, I think we need to turn away from the film's most striking achievements, the power of its motifs and imagery, the brilliant absurdities of its plot and jokes, or rather keep them in mind while not allowing them to quarrel. We need to relax our critical attention rather than intensify it, and we need to see that in this respect both Buñuel's elegant architecture and his quirky narrative are ingredients rather than results. Through them we glimpse, I suggest, not the phantom of liberty but the faint blur of its reality. If we are distracted enough, obtuse enough, we shall understand, perhaps without fully articulating our view, that *The Phantom of Liberty*, like the person who cries 'Long live our chains', is practicing a complicated irony. The film and the phrase declare not a love of constraint but a fear of freedom. Such a fear is often justified and may for many simply be unshakeable. But it is not a destiny, and to learn this is to learn a great deal.

III

I return now to our first, old habit in the cinema, the distraction we think we (distractedly) know, and to a film I have already mentioned, Clint Eastwood's *The Outlaw Josey Wales* (1976). Genre, I suggested earlier, often mirrors and contradicts itself. In one sense it must mirror itself if it is to be a genre, and the recognition of such effects is always going to be partly a result of distraction. To put the matter crudely, if readers of *Paradise Lost* have no sense of the poem as an epic, no memories, however vague, of Homer and Virgil, they will miss half the poem. Yet this sense and these memories are not in the forefront of the reader's mind, as Milton's plot and syntax and metaphors are.

Kafka offers a wonderful insight into this subject. Citing the sentence 'But then he returned to his work, just as though nothing had happened', he says 'This is a remark we are familiar with from a vague profusion of old stories, although perhaps it does not occur in any one of them'.[85] That is the mark of genre: we feel we have been here before, whether we have or we haven't. And vague memories, even erroneous memories, if they are active and literary, may get us deeper into *Paradise Lost* than diligent but alienated seeking in the footnotes.

The Outlaw Josey Wales is based on and closely follows a novel by Forrest Carter called *Gone to Texas*. Wales, a poor farmer in Missouri at the close of the Civil War, sees smoke rising from his house as he ploughs a field. He races home to find the place a mass of flames, and his wife and child dead. His plight is repeatedly compared to that of dispossessed Native Americans, and late in the film, making a personal peace with an Indian Chief, Wales says 'Dying ain't so hard for people like you and me. It's living that's hard, when all you've ever cared for has been butchered and raped'. It is because dying isn't hard for him that killing becomes so easy for Wales, and he becomes so good at it. He's 'not a hard man to track', another character says. 'Leaves dead men wherever he goes'.

Wales has joined a bunch of desperadoes fighting for the South in the last flickers of the Civil War. The novel makes clear he gains a lot of killing experience here, the film allows us to guess this. We see just the tail-end of his membership of the band, which surrenders in return for a notional pardon, only to get massacred. Wales doesn't surrender, he takes off for the South West. And he has two major enemies/targets now: Terrill, the man who raped his wife and killed his child; Fletcher, the leader of the rebel band, the man who sold his men's lives for money.

We know quite a few things about what will happen in the film now. We know it belongs to two narrative or thematic spaces within the western genre: the revenge tale, and the varieties of law in the lawless West. We know that revenge will be achieved; we know that some sort of moral code will prevail, even before we hear our hero announce that 'Doin' right ain't got no end'. We know, to take a trivial example of our knowledge, that when Wales spits his chewed tobacco at someone or something, he will never miss. And we know that no one will be quick enough on the draw to kill him, in spite of the series of attempts that structures the film. The work does not rely on probability or destiny; just the rules of the game. This is where distraction helps a lot. If we concentrate on knowledge of this kind or flaunt it, we are mere pedants. And if we don't have it, we are probably watching the wrong movie. 'Let's not overthink this', is Eastwood's own mantra for his work. He is not saying we should not think, only that we have a habit of doing more thinking than we need to.
Of course the best moments in the film are those where knowledge of

the genre is both relied on and tested. A small example is the point where someone says to Wales, thinking of his pursuers, 'Maybe they'll forget you'. I certainly expect (even though I now know better) that Wales will say something like, 'Maybe so. But I won't forget them'. What he says is a good deal ampler and more philosophical: 'You know there ain't no forgetting'.

I want to look at two instances of genre expectation where, as it happens, the film, written by Phil Kaufman and Sonia Chernus, diverges from the novel. In the first moment, our distracted knowledge is both tested and confirmed; what matters is the stylishness of the confirmation. In the second, it prepares the ground for a surprise.

The first scene is the one that includes the remark I have already quoted, a rare dry comment in the film that is not the contribution of the novelist Forrest Carter: 'Dyin' ain't much of a livin', boy'. The set-up is this. Various groups or individuals have tried to capture or kill Josey Wales and collect the handsome reward – Wales pronounces it ree-ward – for bringing in this wanted man or proving he is dead. The last but one in the series of pursuers, arriving in a ghost town where Wales has made some friends, stares at the outlaw from just inside the door of a saloon, and says 'You're wanted, Wales'. Wales, never a man to miss the chance of a wisecrack, drawls in reply, 'Reckon I'm right popular'. This exchange occurs in both book and film.

In the film Wales asks the man whether he is a bounty hunter, and his answer is 'A man's got to do somethin' for a livin' these days'. This is where Wales makes his remark about dying, and it's worth pausing over the intricate wit of these seemingly casual remarks. The man, not seriously of course but as a matter of notional dignity, pretends bounty hunting is a job like any other. Wales almost imperceptibly translates one life-related idiom into another: making a living into staying alive. We also note the wry understatement of his proposal: 'ain't much of' means 'bears not the faintest resemblance to'. For all the supposedly raw atmosphere of the Old West the spoken words of both men are more like verbal ballet than direct speech. The undeclared content of the conversation consists of a fake excuse for killing followed by a real threat to kill.

The indirection continues. Wales says, quite kindly, 'You know this isn't necessary. You can just ride on'. The man thinks about this, turns and rushes out of the saloon. The worried faces of Wales' friends relax but Wales himself just waits. The man returns. He says, 'I had to come back'. Wales says, 'I know' The man goes for his gun. He's very fast, nearly as fast as Wales. But only nearly. The next minute he is dead.

Our distracted knowledge is very exact here. We know why the man had to come back and we know why Wales was waiting for him to do this. The novel goes out of its way to explain what it is that we and Wales know – perhaps none of us had seen enough Westerns in 1973:

> He knew, once a pistolman was broken, he was walking dead; the nerve gone and reputation shattered. He wouldn't last past the story of his breaking, which would always go ahead of him wherever he went.[86]

This is a plausible, hard-boiled bit of wisdom, but it is far from the only possible reading of what the man finds necessary. Perhaps his idea of honour is less practical and prophetic: he can't leave and still respect himself. Perhaps he has many, conflicting motivations. Perhaps he himself and Wales don't really understand what they are. None of this matters. What matters is the knowledge of what has to happen, not the reasons. We also know that any attempt to fudge this scene, to have it turn out another way, would have been a disaster. The outcome is not optional here but the style and the timing are. Generic destiny can't be defeated but it can be performed in all kinds of ways.

The second scene from *The Outlaw Josey Wales* almost contradicts this claim, falling short only because the issues it addresses are so vast. The issues are revenge and the termination of war. The obvious question is how could revenge not be accomplished in a revenge movie? It is accomplished in *The Outlaw Josey Wales* – or at least one branch of it is. Wales finally meets up with Terrill, the murderer of his wife and child, and swiftly kills him. But what about Fletcher, the man who sold his rebel soldiers to the Union and to their death? Our distracted expertise is really stretched here. Does treachery call for the same class of revenge as butchery? Does revenge recognize such distinctions?

At a late moment in the novel a pair of Texas Rangers, also hunting Wales but on behalf of the law rather than for their profit, discuss their quest with Wales' friends in the ghost-town saloon. The friends all swear not only that Wales is dead but that they have seen him die, and sign a document certifying the fact. Wales himself is also in the saloon, showing no sign of what must be his dry amusement, and quite willing to be addressed as Mr Wells. The Rangers are contented or pretend to be contented, and ride off with their piece of paper.

In the film the traitorous Fletcher is in the room with the Rangers. He says nothing, scarcely shows his disbelief, and certainly reveals no emotion. He can't not have recognized Wales, and he is the person who much earlier in the film responded to a rumour of Wales' death with words of definitive rage: 'I don't want to hear Wales dead, I want to see Wales dead'. He leaves the saloon in the wake of the Rangers with their piece of paper, as Wales does too. Fletcher pauses on the porch of the building and says he doesn't believe the story about Wales' death.

At this point the distracted and the undistracted examiner are likely to have exactly the same expectations, but we do need the contribution of both. There has to be a confrontation, and it has to be elaborate, spectacular in a way the encounter with Terrill was not. In a really dark, later Western, perhaps Wales would die, or both men would die; but here, in 1976, Wales has to win and ride off into the sunset. In the event, he rides off unharmed; but he doesn't win or lose, and Fletcher is unharmed too.

What has happened in this magnificent piece of film writing and directing and acting – nothing like this occurs in the novel – is that the shadows of the Civil War and the wars against the Native Americans have concentrated themselves in the private story of Josey Wales, and an entirely new question has replaced the project of revenge and punishment. The question is whether a war can ever end, especially if it is a justified war.

Continuing his reflection on Wales' non-death, Fletcher says, 'I think I'll go down to Mexico and try to find him'. Wales says, 'And then?' Fletcher says, 'He's got the first move. I owe him that. I think I'll try to tell him the war is over. What do you say, Mr Wilson?' (in the film Wales is temporarily called Wilson rather than Wells). After a long pause Wales says, 'I reckon so. I guess we all died a little in that damn war'. He walks past Fletcher and prepares to mount his horse. He has turned away from his enemy and presents an easy target.

Both our examiners are pretty sure this is where the cowardly Fletcher shoots our hero in the back. A lousy end to the film but sometimes probability (or pessimism) does trump genre and narrative decorum. But then gradually we realize what Wales is doing, and as time passes without a shot we know he is right. He is risking the life he has long been willing to lose, giving Fletcher the chance to underline his villainy one more time, and more astonishingly, since Fletcher does nothing, proving that war and vengeance can find an end beyond endless killing. Both men have honorably refused violence in a world where violence often means honour. Wales departs, and the film ends with a calm, slow shot of the relieved faces of Fletcher and the friends Wales leaves behind.

EPILOGUE

Don't Say Goodbye

I often think, as I watch so many car drivers ignoring road signs, that this may not be mere fecklessness on their part. There is something about verbal signs that presupposes not only attention but a sustained habit of reading. Even if you have no such habit you presumably recognize STOP as a certain shape, in the same way you recognize a speed limit as a number. But why would you attend to every single sign that says DO NOT PASS ON SHOULDER or LIGHTS ON WHEN RAINING or HILL BLOCKS VIEW? You are supposed to be driving not reading.

Still, for those of us for whom language is a career and a passion – the habit of distraction can also be a quiet passion – road signs are both practical instructions and invitations to reverie. We know what HIDDEN DRIVES means and we watch for emerging traffic – but can Freud be far away, and isn't it important to think about those concealments? If I see DO NOT CROSS PAINTED ISLANDS (in New Jersey) or UN TRAIN PEUT EN CACHER UN AUTRE (in Ardèche or Charente), I stay in the indicated lane and I take care at the crossing. But how could I not also think of the wisdom, almost always infringed, of not crossing the painted islands of the mind? How could I not agree that metaphorical trains (of thought, for example) are very likely to mask others of their kind?

The sign with which I wish to close this book has similar associational reaches but is less speculative. I read END OF DIVERSION and I know what I am supposed to think – and do think. I am back on the right road, or at least proceeding unhindered in the right direction. I'm pleased to hear this, I have no quarrel in practice with the good news.

But I can't ignore the leave-taking melancholy in the announcement, a mood that lurks in so many human occasions. End of diversion. The party's over; respectable, responsible life sets in again. What if we were happy on the wrong road, saw unforgettable things in the landscape we had not planned to visit?

Montaigne found diversion a useful tactic, an excellent way of dealing with sorrow or worry. Pascal wasn't really answering him; he was echoing him with a different verdict. He wanted us to concentrate on our misery. What I am calling distraction, what surfaces for me when an end of diversion is proclaimed, is really quite different from both of these gestures, neither a palliative nor an evasion, but . . .

I know diversions have to end, and I'm sure we need quite a few habits that are the reverse of distraction. But I like to imagine that diversion's demise might be provisional, recurring, not a final arrival at the only way. We could attend to our distractions (or find new ones) not because we need them but because we don't, because we are free to think of them. This chance seems to especially important in the realm of interpretation, where what Henry James called 'the possible other case' – another tempo, another reading – keeps crying out for consideration.[87]

Abbreviations

Page references for the following works are given in the text:

Roland Barthes
Oeuvres complètes I–III, Seuil, 1993–1995 (OC).
The Responsibility of Forms, translated by Richard Howard. Blackwell, 1986 (RF).
La Chambre claire. Gallimard/Seuil, 1980 (CC).
Camera Lucida, translated by Richard Howard. Cape, 1982 (CL).

Walter Benjamin
Illuminationen. Suhrkamp, 1977 (I).
Berliner Kindheit. Suhrkamp, 1983 (K).
Selected Writings, volumes 1–4. Harvard, 2003 (SW).

James Joyce
Finnegans Wake. Penguin, 1976 (Wake).

Friedrich Nietzsche
Die fröhliche Wissenschaft. Insel, 2000 (FW).
The Gay Science. Translated by Josefine Nauckhoff. Cambridge, 2001 (GS).

Marcel Proust
Contre Sainte-Beuve. Gallimard 1971 (CSB)
A la recherche du temps perdu I–IV. Gallimard, 1987–1989 (Recherche).
In Search of Lost Time, several translators. Allen Lane, 2002 (Search).

W. B. Yeats
Collected Poems. Macmillan, 1993 (CP).

Notes

1 See p. viii of this book.
2 Siegfried Kracauer, *Das Ornament der Masse*. Surhrkamp, 1963, p. 312.
3 Ibid., pp. 313, 281, 280.
4 Ibid., p. 316.
5 T. W. Adorno, in Walter Benjamin, *Ecrits français*. Gallimard, 1991, pp. 172, 174.
6 Blaise Pascal, *Pensées*. Translated by A. J. Krailsheimer. Penguin, 1995, p. 19.
7 *Ecrits français*, p. 173.
8 I. A. Richards, *Principles of Literary Criticism*. Routledge, 2001, pp. 189, 217.
9 Howard Eiland, 'Reception in Distraction', *Boundary 2*, 30:1, 2003.
10 Miriam Hansen, *Cinema and Experience*. California 2012, p. 86.
11 Jonathan Crary, *Suspensions of Perception*. MIT, 2001, pp. 49, 1.
12 Franz Kafka, *Hochzeitsvorbereitungen auf dem Lande*. Fischer, 1991, p. 62.
13 Franz Kakfa, *Sämtliche Erzählungen*. Fischer, 1982, p. 287. English version in *The Great Wall of China*. Translated by Malcolm Pasley. Penguin, 1973, p. 49.
14 Ibid., p. 287. *The Great Wall*, p. 49.
15 Paul North, *The Problem of Distraction*. Stanford, 2012, pp. 144, 2, 7.
16 Daniel Kahneman, *Thinking Fast and Slow*. Farrar, Straus and Giroux, 2011, p. 23.
17 Michael Warner, 'Uncritical Reading', in Jane Gallop, ed., *Polemic*. Routledge, 2004, p. 33.
18 Tiphaine Samoyault, *Barthes*. Translated by Andrew Brown. Polity, 2016, p. 6.
19 Ibid., p. 4.
20 W. H. Auden, *The Dyer's Hand*. Vintage, 1989, p. 325.
21 David Ulin, *The Lost Art of Reading*. Sasquatch, 2010, pp. 150, 4, 76, 54, 34.
22 Roland Barthes, *Le plaisir du texte*. Seuil, 1973, p. 41. *The Pleasure of the Text*. Translated by Richard Miller. Hill and Wang, 1974, p. 24.
23 Ibid., pp. 18–19.
24 Roland Barthes, *Fragments d'un discours amoureux*. In *Oeuvres complètes 3*, p. 516.
25 *Roland Barthes par Roland Barthes*. Seuil, 1975, p. 90.

26 Bertolt Brecht, *Poems 1913–1956*. Methuen, 1987, p. 328.

27 Roland Barthes, *Le plaisir du texte*, p. 70; S/Z. Seuil, 1970, p. 104.

28 John Sturrock, *Structuralism and Since*. Oxford, 1979, p. 61.

29 Roland Barthes, *L'Empire des signes*. Skira, 1970, pp. 91, 98, 13.

30 Ibid., p. 123.

31 Jacques Lacan, *Ecrits*. Translated by Bruce Fink. Norton, 2004, p. 57.

32 Marina van Zuylen, *The Plenitude of Distraction*. Sequence, 2017, pp. 3–31.

33 Søren Kierkegaard, *Either/Or*, Part I. Princeton, 1987, p. 299.

34 *Cinema and Experience*, p. 292.

35 John Ruskin, *The Stones of Venice volume 2*. CreateSpace, 2015, p. 118.

36 A Conan Doyle, *A Scandal in Bohemia*. In *The Complete Sherlock Holmes, volume 3*. Barnes and Noble, 2003, p. 79.

37 *The Stones of Venice volume 2*, pp. 118–119.

38 Douglas Mao, *Fateful Beauty*. Princeton, 2008, pp. 5, 4, 44.

39 Marcel Proust, *Jean Santeuil*. Gallimard, 1971, p. 537.

40 Walter Benjamin, *Sur Proust*. Nous, 2010, p. 105.

41 Rebecca Comay, 'Benjamin's Endgame'. In *Walter Benjamin's Philosophy*, ed. Andrew Benjamin. Routledge, 1993, p. 266.

42 *Sur Proust*, pp. 105–106.

43 Carolin Duttlinger, 'Between Contemplation and Distraction', *German Studies Review* 30:1, 2007.

44 Quoted in Henning Teschke, *Proust und Benjamin*. Königshausen und Neumann, 2000, p. 111.

45 Henry James, Letter to Howard Sturgis, quoted in F. W. Dupee, *Henry James*. Delta, 1965, pp. 248–249.

46 Friedrich Nietzsche, *The Birth of Tragedy and the Genealogy of Morals*. Translated by Francis Golffing. Doubleday, 1956, p. 149.

47 *Miles Davis: the Autobiography*. Macmillan, 1989, p. 389.

48 *Birth of the Cool*. CD, 1989.

49 Richard Williams, *The Blue Moment*. Faber, 2009, p. 51.

50 Farah Jasmine Griffin and Salim Washington, *Clawing at the Limits of the Cool*. St Martin's, 2008, subtitle.

51 Ibid., pp. 11–13.

52 Ibid., p. 10.

53 Eric Nisenson, *The Making of Kind of Blue*. St Martin's Press, 2000, p. 214.

54 *Miles Davis: the Autobiography*, p. 224.

55 *The Blue Moment*, p. 118.

56 *Miles Davis: The Autobiography*, p. 73.

57 *Clawing at the Limits of the Cool*, p. 3.

58 Ralph Ellison, *Living with Music*. Modern Library, 2002, p. 103.

59 Peter Pettinger, *Bill Evans*. Yale, 1998, p. 82.

60 *Miles Davis: the Autobiography*, p. 224.
61 Ibid., p. 216.
62 D. A. Miller, *Hidden Hitchcock*. Chicago, 2016, p. 157.
63 Ibid., p. 4.
64 Ibid., p. 11.
65 Ibid., p. 8.
66 Edward W. Said, *Musical Elaborations*. Chatto & Windus, 1991, p. 105.
67 Keith M May, *Nietzsche and Modern Literature*. Macmillan, 1988, p. 18.
68 Roy Foster, *W. B. Yeats II*. Oxford, 2003, p. 553.
69 Paul de Man, 'Sign and Symbol in Hegel's *Aesthetics*'. *Critical Inquiry 13*, 1982.
70 Rei Terada, *Looking Away*. Harvard, 2009, p. 115.
71 Thomas Hobbes, *The Elements of Law*. CreateSpace, 2017, 26.
72 F. Scott Fitzgerald, *This Side of Paradise*. CreateSpace, 2017, p. 5.
73 T. S. Eliot, 'The Love Song of J Alfred Prufrock'. In *Collected Poems*. Harcourt Brace Jovanovich, 1991, pp. 3, 4.
74 Christopher Ricks, *T. S. Eliot and Prejudice*. Faber, 1994, pp. 16, 18.
75 Ibid., pp. 14, 16.
76 Roy Foster, *W. B. Yeats II*, p. 550.
77 W. B. Yeats, *Letters on Poetry to Dorothy Wellesley*. Littlefield, 2007, p. 9.
78 John Russell, *Max Ernst*. Thames and Hudson, 1967, p. 126.
79 J. G. Ballard, *The Drowned World*. Liveright, 2013, p. 41.
80 Uwe M. Schneede, *Max Ernst*. Translated by R. W. Last. Praeger, 1973, p. 168.
81 Howard Eiland and Michael Jennings, *Walter Benjamin*. Harvard, 2014, pp. 640, 605.
82 Luis Buñuel, *Mon dernier soupir*. Laffont, 1982, p. 307.
83 Joan Mellen, 'The Phantom of Liberty', in Joan Mellen, ed., *The World of Luis Buñuel*. Oxford, 1978, p. 331.
84 Maurice Drouzy, *Luis Buñuel*. Lherminier, 1978, p. 244.
85 *Hochzeitsvorbereitungen auf dem Lande*, p. 40. *The Great Wall of China*, p. 98.
86 Forrest Carter, *Gone to Texas*. University of New Mexico, 1989, p. 191.
87 Henry James, *The Art of Fiction*. Chicago, 2011, p. 222.

Index

www.ingramcontent.com/pod-product-compliance
Lightning Source LLC
Chambersburg PA
CBHW052013270326
41929CB00015B/2900